The
Nick
Murray
Reader

Other books by Nick Murray

for advisors
> *The New Financial Advisor*

for clients
> *Simple Wealth, Inevitable Wealth*

for wholesalers
> *On Becoming A Great Wholesaler*

The Nick Murray Company, Inc.
P.O. Box 1554
Mattituck, NY 11952
Phone: 631-298-1840
Fax: 631-298-1845
www.nickmurray.com

Printed in the United States of America

Library of Congress Control Number: 2003106575
ISBN: 0-9669763-3-9

This book is for my editor,

my most astute critic,

my daughter

Karen Elizabeth Murray

That which has been is what will be, that which is done is what will be done, and there is nothing new under the sun.
  – *Ecclesiastes 1:9*

There is nothing new in the world except the history you do not know.
  – *Harry S Truman*

There is no remembrance of former things, nor will there be any remembrance of things that are to come by those who will come after.
  – *Ecclesiastes 1:11*

"This time is different" are among the most costly four words in market history.
  – *Sir John Templeton*

FOREWORD

This is a collection of some four dozen essays which appeared, between the end of 1999 and the middle of 2003, in one of three places: the Canadian magazine *Advisor's Edge*, the American magazine *Financial Advisor*, or my newsletter/spot coaching service, *Nick Murray Interactive*.

The *Advisor's Edge* essays have never been seen in this country at all. The *Financial Advisor* essays have never been archived. And the newsletter pieces have hitherto been archived only for subscribers.

These essays are interspersed with about three dozen Q&A pieces – real questions from real advisors, and my responses – on everything from market conditions to practice management to the handling of difficult clients and prospects.

The first few essays deal with the mass manias of Y2K and the tech bubble. The last few address the runup to Operation Iraqi Freedom, and the outlook after its spectacularly successful conclusion. In between, I tried – month by month, as the horrors unfolded – to help advisors deal appropriately with the terrorist atrocities of September 11, and with the longest, deepest bear market since the 1930s.

This book is intended to be a companion and a supplement to *The New Financial Advisor*. *TNFA* is a complete system for formulating and executing a great career as a financial advisor, regardless of the rise and fall of economies, markets and current events. *The Nick Murray Reader*, on the other hand, is an unstructured, unsystematic (though chronological) collection of real-world observations and coaching. I hope the reader will find value in dipping into it whenever the occasion arises, and in returning to specific situational advice on issues he or she may be facing on any given day. Above all, I hope the totality of this book will serve as an object lesson in keeping the faith.

I am whatever I am, and can do whatever good I do, because of the love and support of my family: my wife Joan, my daughter Joan Eileen, my son Mark, and the young woman to whom this book is dedicated. Just this morning, it seems, she was a warm spring rain of a girl, running out the door to go sailing with her little friends. But when I came home tonight, she had somehow become my grandchildren's mother. And, being her own mother's daughter, what a mother she is.

Y2K, THE BOOK OF REVELATION AND THE APOCALYPSE *DU JOUR*: NOTES ON THE PERSISTENCE OF PESSIMISM

(By October 1999, as the Y2K hysteria mounted, I was hearing from a lot of advisors who were looking for a rigorous intellectual rebuttal. I didn't think the issue was the least bit intellectual, and tried in this piece to demonstrate why. It helped a lot that I'd been reading Robert Lacey and Danny Danziger's wonderful book The Year 1000, *which is where the information on the first millennium came from.)*

In a study of one thousand mutual fund investors published at mid-year 1999, 39% said they were "highly concerned" about the so-called Y2K computer issues, and 14% stated categorically that they would sell fund shares by December because of Y2K.

What are we as investment advisors to make of this millennial mass mania, and what does it tell us of the deep need among investors serially to fear whatever apocalypse *du jour* – real or imagined – comes to hand?

Harry Truman said that the only thing new in the world is the history that you do not know. Thus, we can learn a lot about the abnormal psychology surrounding the millennium bug if we look closely at – you guessed it – the first millennium.

Starting in the year 989 with the frightening appearance

of what we now know was Halley's comet, the run-up to the year 1000 was marked throughout western Europe by a growing conviction that a particular prophecy in the Book of Revelation meant the end was nigh. St. John wrote, in Revelation 20:1-3, that Christ's coming had chained Satan up for a thousand years. Western theologians decided that this meant the devil would reappear with a vengeance at millennium midnight.

Well, the millennium came and went; the end of the world did not take place. Whereupon everyone started worrying that the cataclysm would happen in the year 1033, on the thesis that Satan's thousand-year jail term didn't start until Jesus's death and resurrection at age 33.

We're still at it. Only this time it's not Satan we worry about, but the HAL 9000 computer from Stanley Kubrick's classic film *2001: A Space Odyssey*. Remember? HAL 9000 was the spaceship supercomputer that went psychotic and killed all but one of the human crew before the lone survivor lobotomized it. Who can ever forget their famous colloquy: "Open the pod bay doors, HAL." "I'm sorry, Dave, I'm afraid I can't do that."

It's useless, and even counterproductive, to try to reason out the facts of Y2K with victims of millennium mania. Worth noting, however, is that fact that no "crisis" which gives as much advance warning as did this one ever turns out to be a real crisis. The issue was never whether the problem was going to get fixed – of course it was going to get fixed – but how much fixing it might cost in corporate earnings, government expenditures and diminished economic growth. With growth and earnings continuing to roar – at a time when most of what's going to be spent fixing the problem has already been spent – Y2K may be shaping up to be the non-event of the millennium.

Much more interesting than the facts of the matter is what millennium mania says about human nature, and about the terrible craving that many people have to believe in the inevitability of some sort of crash. Then again, the apocalypse *du jour* may simply be a proxy for something entirely different that's bothering your client/prospect – something as simple (but unspeakable) as, "I just don't know if I can trust you."

Try to shrink the problem down to manageable proportions by asking specifically what the investor fears might happen *to him*. For example, as long as he's got his November statement, his securities and cash balances can't disappear.

Moreover, in addition to your reassurances, the investor can get further comfort from his banker, his mutual fund sponsors, and even the NYSE, with a few quick phone calls.

By refocusing the issue on what it really is – the value of your advice – you stand your best chance of keeping people moving toward their long-term goals.

– *Advisor's Edge,* October 1999

NOTES ON THE BUBBLE

(For all the good it did me, by the first quarter of 2000 I felt we were in the grip of the greatest financial bubble in human history, and that substantially all the money that had gone into dot.com IPOs since the beginning of 1999 was about to be lost. And I said so in my Advisor's Edge *columns of February and April – as it turned out, just before and just after the market cracked.*

I say "for all the good it did me" because there's no greater torture in investing than knowing what's going to happen and not knowing when. As Peter Lynch famously said, "Far more money has been lost by investors in preparing for corrections, or anticipating corrections, than has been lost in the corrections themselves."

The only thing harder than getting out of the market at the right time is getting back in opportunely; since I've long since become convinced that no one can consistently do either, I'm stuck with "buy and hold." Or, more accurately, "buy and keep buying" – the patient accumulator's mantra.

I reprint these two pieces here because they may serve to remind the advisor of three timeless truths. First, that she is never of greater potential value to clients than at market extremes, when the temptation to make The Big Mistake is strongest. Second, that the ultimate irony of all great technological revolutions is that the technology succeeds, but investments in the first few years of that technology don't.

And finally, that the advisor always has the right – and perhaps even the moral duty – not to accept a client's suicidally speculative order.)

AND YET AGAIN, THE TULIPS BLOOM

Once a year, whether I think I need to or not, I reread the section of Charles Mackay's 1841 classic book *Extraordinary Popular Delusions and the Madness of Crowds* which deals with the Tulip Mania.

This was the great financial craze which burst forth in Holland in the winter of 1636-37, when the objects of speculation were all very conveniently under the earth, and could not even be examined by buyers or sellers. (The maniacs weren't trading tulip bulbs at all, but rather tulip bulb *futures*.)

This winter, it's happening again. Only this time it's Internet stocks. That, however, is not quite the point of this essay. The point is: in the great cycle of euphoria and terror that is the never-changing history of markets, *it's always something.*

Don't get me wrong: I love the Internet. I agree with Netscape founder Jim Clark, who said (nearly five years ago, when no one – including Bill Gates – was listening), "The Internet is the future of all data communication, and all communications are data communications."

And I agree almost exactly with GE's Jack Welch, who in March of 1999 called the web "the single most important event in the U.S. economy since the Industrial Revolution." Except that I'd have said "in the *world* economy."

But the Internet stock market mania has nothing whatever to do with the Internet, any more than the Tulip Mania had anything to do with tulip bulbs.

Virtually all great technological breakthroughs spawn an intense burst of start-up entrepreneurial activity, fueled by a tidal wave of capital eager to profit from the new miracle. In the 20th century alone, at least five such earth-shaking developments preceded the Internet: the automobile, the airplane, radio, television and the microprocessor.

About 500 auto makers were incorporated in the U.S. from 1900 to 1910; three remain. The sum of all net earnings in the airline industry from Orville Wright's flight at Kitty Hawk in 1903 through the same date in 1999 is zero. There are more television sets in America today than ever before – but no American TV manufacturers. Remember your first desktop microchip-powered calculator? *Sic transit gloria* Commodore.

Like all five of the previously cited innovations, the Internet is here to stay. It will continue profoundly to influence the life of the world, in ways we perhaps may not yet dream of. (It took 44 years to get from Kitty Hawk through the sound barrier, but only 22 more to get to the moon.)

And, of course, the greater part of the capital that's been invested in the Internet since 1995 – including virtually every dollar that's gone into the IPO mania of the last year – is going ultimately to be lost. For this, ladies and gentlemen, is the greatest financial bubble in the history of the world.

But that goes without saying. That always happens. Market manias – and the ensuing market panics – aren't driven by changing technology, but by immutable human nature. In his great book *Reminiscences of a Stock Operator*, Edwin Lefèvre said, "Nowhere does history indulge in repetitions so often or so uniformly as in Wall Street. When you read contemporary accounts of booms or panics, the one thing that strikes you most forcibly is how little either stock speculation or stock speculators today differ from yesterday. The game does not change and neither does human nature." Though these words sound as if they'd been written an hour ago, Lefèvre published them in 1923.

Much as you may be vexed by your clients' susceptibility to this latest incarnation of the madness, remember that this is precisely why investors need us. Illness and injury necessitate the physician; human nature – ever at its worst in financial markets – is why the excellent investment advisor will always be indispensable.

– *Advisor's Edge*, February 2000

RAPTURE OF THE DEEP

Scuba enthusiasts know that one risk of long dives is a condition called nitrogen narcosis – most commonly referred to by the darkly poetic phrase "rapture of the deep."

Nitrogen buildup in the diver's bloodstream produces a particularly delicious euphoria; the victim loses all sense of danger. In a hundred feet of water, he'll simply shed his uncomfortable mask and air hose, or swim away into an unexplored cave and never come out.

Today's advisors are now having to deal with clients afflicted by the investment equivalent of rapture of the deep – a condition I call silicon narcosis. The presenting symptom of this pathology is the conviction that no price is too high to pay for technology stocks in general and Internet stocks in particular.

Moreover, sufferers from silicon narcosis exhibit an enthusiasm for technology stocks which correlates inversely with their intellectual comprehension of the technology. Simply stated, the less the doomed speculators can understand what a company does, the more consuming their passion for the stock.

Note, too, that late-stage silicon narcosis can strike down even clients who've spent most of their investing lifetimes in the serial grip of some or another equally irrational fear (Y2K in 1999, "runaway deflation" the year before that, and so on).

Faced with all this, advisors can be forgiven for feeling totally bereft. Given that our clients spend far more time and energy at the bottom of the terror/euphoria cycle than at the top, most advisors have had no training or experience in treating an extreme speculative recklessness which the victim himself denies he has.

And it gets worse. At least the diving buddy of a nitrogen narcosis sufferer may get him to the surface and back in the boat, out of harm's way. But you and I can't, in good conscience, take people completely out of equities. The first rule of lifetime equity investing is that you have to stay in it to win it.

Even advisors who rationalize going to the sidelines on the thesis that the bursting of the dot.com bubble will start a bear market may already be too late. On anything but a cap-weighted basis, we've been in a bear market for months.

By late February, the average stock in the S&P 500 was off 31% from its 52-week high. The average Nasdaq stock – even as the cap-weighted index itself hit new highs – was off 30%. (This tells you there are actually two U.S. stock markets: one a speculative silicon lunatic asylum, and one a not unreasonably priced garden of value.)

The challenge is not to guess when the bubble will burst –

that's not investing, it's musical chairs. The challenge is to remind clients that they came into this race to be the tortoise who always wins, at a moment when every fiber of their being is screaming to be a hare.

Ultimately, the advisor's best antidote to silicon narcosis isn't intellectual. (You can no more reason with euphoria than with fear: either way, the victim says, "This time it's different.") The serum is moral: you can – and you must – refuse to take the order.

I always told clients I anticipated meeting with their family the afternoon of their funeral, to explain what we'd done. And I'd refuse an order I thought suicidal by saying, "I wouldn't be able to explain this. I couldn't tell them I knew it was wrong but I let you do it anyway. So please do this, if you must, with another advisor, or online."

Sometimes that'll get 'em back in the boat. Sometimes it won't. But you'll have done the right thing. And that's my definition of success.

– *Advisor's Edge*, April 2000

MONEY IS LOVE

Money is love. In that sense, it's a force of nature. And, like any force of nature, it can be both powerfully constructive and terribly destructive.

Electricity warms and lights your home; it can also electrocute you. Water sustains your life, and it can drown you. Money is love, but it can also be – and not infrequently is – used to express love's absence, and even love's opposite.

In our profession, when mediocrity thinks about money, it automatically thinks about markets and investments: whither interest rates, or has Japan bottomed, or will Mutual Fund Raindrop A get to the bottom of the window before Mutual Fund Raindrop B. Thus, in its perfect genius for missing the essential point, mediocrity focuses on variables which are both unknowable and of no critical consequence to a family's financial life.

Excellence knows that in every family dynamic it encounters, money is an expression – for good or ill – of the relationship among the family's members.

Where it concludes that money is being used to propagate the family dysfunction ("Never mind estate planning; my kids are rotten and I'm not leaving them anything"), excellence takes a walk.

It's very difficult to serve genuinely mean-spirited people well. They don't really want you to (because they know they don't deserve it), and will turn their nastiness on you if you try. For example, people who don't love their children don't love anyone, and will one day not love you – with a vengeance. (And the younger the advisor, the sooner the dysfunctional parent will make him or her a proxy for the children.)

But where it discovers a reasonably healthy money dynamic, excellence asks three questions, which are intended to discover how the money seeks to express the love.

These questions are, of course: who is the money for, what is the money for, and when will the money be needed?

Excellence invests a lot of time and energy getting shared agreement throughout the family on the answers to these questions. Next, it crafts a comprehensive plan for the realization of the family's goals – and again gets a conceptual sign-off from all the adults concerned. Then, and only then, does it address tertiary issues such as what specific investments will be used to fund the plan.

Once more, reading from top to bottom, the excellent agenda is: the love, then the plan, and then the investments.

Mediocrity unerringly signals its presence by going to the third issue first. Its excuse is that that's what the prospect asked about. But again, what people *want* to talk about is usually the opposite of what they *need* to talk about. And reacting to the prospect's agenda instead of resetting it in healthier terms is mediocrity's art form.

It's quite common for people to ask me what I think of the market, or of a particular mutual fund. These are the wrong questions. It's very rare for people to ask me how they can construct an income they can't outlive, so they'll be able to maintain dignity and independence in old age, and not burden the children they love. This is among the very few right questions.

Mediocrity guesses at answers to the wrong questions. Excellence gently guides people to the right questions. ("This money that you're thinking of investing in the market/the fund *du jour*: may I ask you, who is it for, what is it for, and when will it be needed?") Mediocrity makes statements it can't prove; excellence asks wonderful questions.

Excellence knows that, in the end, it can only help people who genuinely want to be helped. And that it *should* help only people who deserve to be helped.

– *Advisor's Edge*, January 1999

THE SHOEMAKER'S CHILDREN

Not too long ago, a phenomenally successful American life insurance agent and his wife were planning a European vacation. This was a man who had built not only his career but an entire agency on comprehensive estate planning. The only problem was that he himself didn't even have a will.

His wife's position on the matter was clear: she wouldn't get on the plane with him unless the situation were remedied. So just before they left, he knocked out a simple boilerplate will on some financial planning software he had at home. He got it witnessed, and stuck it in his desk drawer.

The next evening, the couple boarded TWA flight 800 from New York's JFK airport to Paris. Half an hour after takeoff, they and everyone else on the plane were dead.

That was, for me, only the most extreme example of a very common phenomenon in our profession: the fabled shoemaker's children who go barefoot.

Beyond the obvious point that this is an awful thing to do to oneself and one's family, I wonder that we do not see how infinitely more effective we become by practicing what we preach.

How can I get people to buy and hold equity mutual funds

when I myself am stock-picking and – worse – trading the stocks I pick? How can I convince people to dollar-cost average when I'm trying to time the market in my own account? How will I persuade people to make a comprehensive financial/investment/estate plan when I've provided my own family with none?

My answer to all these questions is the same: I can't. Soon or late, real clients are moved not by what we say but by who we are. And we are what we do: this is the iron rule of excellence. Mediocrity manages money; excellence leads people – and ultimately finds that it can only lead by example.

This is not merely another way of saying that we're much more effective convincing investors to buy things we ourselves own (or at least would own). That axiom is certainly true as far as it goes, but it doesn't go nearly far enough, because it focuses on the wrong variable.

Lifetime investment success is not, as I've said before, driven by investment "performance." No one will achieve or fail to achieve financial independence because he owns Growth Fund A instead of Growth Fund B. Rather, financial success is a product of appropriate investor behavior. And we will not, at the end of the day, be able to convince large numbers of people to behave better than we do.

If you would induce prospective clients to be open and honest with you about their financial situations, their goals, dreams, hopes and fears, be willing (within reason) to share yours with them. If they're reluctant to put your more difficult (but most necessary) recommendations into action, offer them some insight into your own struggles. Don't instruct; *empathize.*

The way to get people to take your financial planning capabilities more seriously is to believe in and practice them more seriously in your own life. So, if you're looking for a way to make yourself quickly and dramatically more effective, take the plunge and start today on your own comprehensive plan. It will make you feel much better about yourself. It will bring you much closer to the people you love. And, not least of all, it will greatly increase your technical understanding of the legal and tax aspects of the planning process, which in turn boosts your self-confidence and credibility.

Like most issues which initially appear to be about professional competence or the fundamentals of practice management, this is really a character issue. Who do you claim you are, and what is your basis for that claim? Mediocrity is an imposter. Excellence is the genuine article. Good clients feel that, and respond in kind.

– *Advisor's Edge*, August 1999

THREE CAUTIONARY NOTES
ON THE ILLUSION OF LOGIC

We should take care not to make the intellect our god;
it has, of course, powerful muscles, but no personality.
– Einstein

Pure logic is the ruin of the spirit.
– Antoine de Saint-Exupéry

A mind all logic is like a knife all blade.
It makes the hand bleed that uses it.
– Rabindranath Tagore

SELLING STEWARDSHIP

One of the world's finest watchmakers is running a series of advertisements the tag line of which is that you never really own a Patek Philippe; you just take care of it for the next generation.

We financial advisors would do well to adapt this philosophy of stewardship to the way we promote and explain the concept of multigenerational wealth.

I recently listened to an excellent presentation by a leading financial planner, in which he intuitively used this approach. His client was a 72-year-old widow who had a 35-year-old son and a 6-year-old granddaughter.

The planner had been called in precisely because the widow wanted to provide the most tax-efficient transfer of her assets to her heirs when she died, while enjoying a solid income from those assets during her remaining lifetime.

When the time came to select a portfolio, the widow and her accountant just assumed the planner would recommend a predominately bond-based approach. Instead, he proposed upwards of 90% equities. He cited two reasons.

The less important factor was that the widow might well need her income to go on rising steadily for another 20 years or more, to keep pace with her increasing living costs.

"But ultimately," the planner continued, pointing to the little girl's picture, "it's her capital we're investing. And she needs you to keep it growing for her." The accountant began to raise another question, but was silenced by the good lady, who had heard exactly what she needed to hear, and knew it.

In my book for clients, *Simple Wealth, Inevitable Wealth*, I counsel investors that they may really appreciate equities only when they begin thinking in multigenerational time.

At the very least, good clients seek to maintain their dignity and independence in retirement; above all, they don't want ever to become a financial burden to their children. In retirements which may last upwards of 30 years, this dictates a primary investment objective of neither growth nor income, but rather growth *of* income.

Growth of income can reliably be derived only from equity investing. The cash dividend of the S&P 500 in 1999, for example, was about 450% of what it was in 1975, but interest rates had declined substantially...while the CPI had roughly tripled.

Moreover, equity investing for growth of income during our own retirements has an even greater benefit. While our incomes rise (well ahead of inflation, historically), our capital is also growing into a significant endowment for succeeding generations of people we love. (While the cash dividend of the S&P is up four and a half times in the last quarter century, the Index itself has risen by a factor of 10.)

You'll find that talking to clients about investing for multigenerational time horizons makes it infinitely easier for them to accept equities. This is simply because the effect of time on equities is so miraculous.

If I had told your father in 1950 that at the millennium you alone would personally command more computing power than existed on earth that year, I'll bet he'd have been more than eager to invest in equities for himself and you. If I'd added that the Dow Jones Industrials (excluding dividends) would rise 50 times in those 50 years, he'd have been even more enthusiastic.

Yet today we feel – quite rightly – that we've only just begun. If the last 2000 years were a 24-hour day, Communism fell eight seconds before midnight, and the Internet rose four seconds after that. What miracles will our children see – and profit from, if we have the wisdom to invest appropriately?

A wonderful ad for a major brokerage firm shows a fortyish father, surrounded by his family, saying, "I want my great-great-grandchildren to come from old money."

Isn't that what we all want for our client families – and for our own?

– *Financial Advisor,* July-August 2000

WISDOM SOLD SEPARATELY

Information is endlessly available
to us; where shall wisdom be found?
— Harold Bloom,
How To Read – And Why

With the obvious exception of the global capitalist revolution itself, the most important development of the last 10 years is the Internet. As the internal combustion engine was the defining technology at the beginning of the last century, surely the web defines the start of this one.

Indeed it is difficult to say where globalizing capitalism leaves off and the web begins. For if, as Michael Rothschild says in his classic book *Bionomics*, capitalism – like DNA – is most efficient as a carrier of information, the Internet represents the total democratization of information: the universal availability, at virtually no cost, of everything that everyone knows. And thus, like capitalism, the web is a force of nature.

In few areas of human endeavor has the net intervened so quickly and dramatically as investing. The staggering quantity of instantly available financial information, and the speed with which the wired individual can act on it, captivated a whole new generation of Internet trading devotees.

That these people did not see that trading is speculating

rather than investing, and that they did not know that portfolio turnover correlates negatively with return, are subjects for another day.

Of much greater and far more terrible consequence was the fact that its adherents didn't seem to realize that the web does not think, nor exercise any judgment. It limitlessly provides all available good information – and bad information – without distinction. It will tell you facts which, properly employed, may lead you to wealth, and which, used badly, will help you destroy yourself. When the stars of Internet trading information include people who call themselves motley fools, we may safely take them at their word. Garbage in, garbage out.

We don't yet forbid the sale of cigarettes in this country, and probably never will. We do, however, blazon on each pack, and on all advertising therefor, the inarguable fact that smoking causes cancer. We don't proscribe the sale of alcoholic beverages, but we post signs in bars and liquor stores warning that pregnant women who drink risk deforming their babies. Just so, I know that we can't – and shouldn't – forbid investors the Internet, nor the personal computer and modem which give them access to it. But there should, I believe, be a cautionary label on each piece of hardware, and the same legend should flash on the screen at least once every minute when you're online. It would say, of course, WARNING: WISDOM SOLD SEPARATELY.

Successful investing is not at all about the information which, since it's universally available on the web, must already be in the price anyway. It's about behavior: the wisdom (or folly) with which one responds to shocking market events that one didn't anticipate. All the web access in the world doesn't seem to have prepared anyone for the mini-crash of August '98, with Russia's default, the Asian meltdown, and Latin America's threat to become the next domino. And no amount of information saved the legions of the newly impoverished who bought one dot.com stock or another on margin through the winter of 1999-2000.

If anything, all that information may have given people a false sense of security. ("If I have all this up-to-date information, am I not totally on top of the markets, and prepared for anything?" Well, as it turned out, no.) The result was to magnify the shock of getting blindsided, increasing the odds of a panicky "sell" decision.

And of course one's Internet broker will never try to talk one out of that (or any other) bad decision. It will do the only thing it can: give people an instant and limitless outlet for all their very worst instincts.

"Electronic wisdom" is an oxymoron. Fortunately, therefore, wisdom is the stock in trade of the excellent financial advisor. No matter how much information may come out of a machine, wisdom never will. Investors will obtain it from us or not at all.

The net has what people want, but we have what they need. So say it loud; say it proud: *wisdom sold separately.*

– *NMI Sample Issue*, Fall 2000

THE LAST WORD ON REFERRALS

In the summer of 1967, when, as a beardless boy, I was in the stockbroker training program of the late, lamented E.F. Hutton & Company, one of the hottest topics of discussion was how to get referrals.

This summer, I was inquiring of a life insurance sales executive the issues he might like me to cover in a talk that I'm doing for his agents. The first topic he came up with was how to get referrals.

You will not have failed to note that a third of a century intervenes between the two foregoing paragraphs.

Now, maybe that just means each new generation has to learn the same skill in its own time, like riding a bicycle. And maybe it just means that new and interesting ways to obtain referrals are constantly presenting themselves, so that the topic is evergreen.

But I don't think so. I think "How do you get referrals?" is like "How do you prospect?" It's a question everybody already knows the answer to, and doesn't like the answer. So we keep asking it, hoping against hope to discover a magical "technique" which will allow us to short-cut the real answer.

The answer to "How do you prospect?" is, of course, to offer your services, with passion and conviction, to enough people. It's always going to be a numbers game, and you just have to be willing to listen to enough people say "no" until enough people have said "yes." It doesn't matter how you prospect; it just matters *that* you prospect, and never stop.

Similarly, there's only one way systematically to get referrals. And that is to make your clients enthusiastic enough about you and your work that they freely and strongly recommend you.

Advisors whose clients are raving fans get all the referrals they need or want, pretty much effortlessly. Advisors whose client relationships are strained, resentful or rife with disappointment (in either or both directions) get few (and similarly flawed) referrals – or none at all.

This is just one more reason (if you still need another) never to put up with difficult clients. Indeed the phrase "difficult clients" is almost a contradiction. Troublesome people are really customers: people who go to the same supermarket every week, complain about the length of the checkout lines – and are back the next week, complaining yet again.

Clients may be distinguished from customers in that clients respect your advice and follow your counsel without carping or excessive second-guessing. As they would with a doctor, they go home and take the medicine you prescribed – for the simple reason that you prescribed it –

believing that they will get better. When they do recover, many become raving fans. And – with gentle, consistent prompting – raving fans can easily be induced to become carriers of the word.

A doctor is confident enough in himself as a humane healer that he expects his patients to follow his advice. He will spend little time and even less energy on a patient who demands to examine his credentials, or to read the government testing studies of the recommended medicine, or to negotiate his fee. And he will certainly not be fool enough to look for referrals from such a head case.

Why are we less confident than the doctor, and therefore more susceptible to wrangling with our "patient"? Is it because we rightly don't believe in the medicine we're prescribing? ("Buy now; the market's about to go up." "The Gronsky Emerging Markets Fund gives you higher returns with less volatility.") If so, the fault lies not in our clients but in ourselves. If not, referrals shouldn't be a problem.

The referral process is: (a) do great work (b) for people who appreciate it and (c) encourage the resulting raving fans to spread the good news. It's not a technique. It's an attitude.

– *Financial Advisor,* November-December 2000

LET THEM FEEL THEIR FEAR

During significant market declines, many advisors try to deal with clients' fears by offering up a variety of tortured statistical analyses of past bear markets, showing how they've always been temporary.

When I ask advisors what their objective is in doing this, the answer is invariably that they're trying to convince the client not to be afraid. Personally, I think this is a big mistake.

Our job isn't to prevent the client from experiencing fear. It's to prevent him from acting on the fear, and that's an entirely different thing.

Fact has never been a particularly useful tool in dealing with fear. If you doubt this, try sitting next to an extreme white-knuckle flyer on your next plane ride. Show him the almost absurdly low statistics on fatalities per passenger mile in airplanes compared to those in automobiles. He not only won't relax in response to your reasoned analysis, but he may prove literally unable to hear what you're saying. *You can't reason with fear.*

Besides, when fear really takes hold, statistical analysis of past bear markets becomes not merely useless but counterproductive, in that it prompts your client to burst into the four-word death song of the American investor: "This time it's different."

The way to deal with fear is to validate it – to respect it as a natural, normal human reaction – and to empathize with it. For it is precisely in the act of giving people permission to feel their fear that we may begin to calm them – and to show them that we ourselves are not afraid.

Client: I think we'd better get out of the market. This (fill in the apocalypse *du jour*) situation isn't going to get resolved any time soon, and a lot of people are saying that the market could go a lot lower. Let's just move into money markets for a while.

Advisor [making no attempt to deal with the stated concern]: Yes, this is a profoundly upsetting kind of experience, particularly when [empathize with the client's unique personal situation] you've never been through anything like it before/you're as close to retirement as you are/you've never had as much of your capital exposed to the equity markets as you do now. I completely understand how you feel. Indeed, you wouldn't be human if you didn't feel this way. [Silence.]

Client: Well, what do you think I should do?

Advisor: I don't think you should do much of anything, but we can talk about that in a minute, if you still want to. For the moment, I was just trying to validate your fears and concerns, and to reassure you that everybody goes through what you're going through when the market turns ugly like this. [Silence.]

Client: Forgive me, but I still don't know what you're advising me to do.

Advisor: I'm advising you to realize that fear of declining markets – especially with the media fueling that fear – is a basic human instinct. I'm also advising you that selling your fundamental, long-term, core investments in response to the fear of some current-events "crisis" or other is something a lot of people do – and end up bitterly regretting. It's OK to feel the fear, but it's not OK to act on the fear. Let me ask you: do you ever remember being as worried about the state of the world as you are now?

Client: Now that you mention it: do you remember before the war in the Gulf started, and they were saying it could be another Vietnam? And there was a recession, and the banking system looked like death, and there was all that talk about layoffs and downsizing. And the deficit; I almost forgot the deficit.

Advisor: And junk bonds, and insider trading.

Client: Right, right. That's probably when I felt the most like I do now.

Advisor: That was late in 1990 – say, the last third of the year.

Client: And where was the market then?

Advisor: Bless your heart; that's exactly the question I hoped you'd ask. And the answer is: around Dow 2500.

Client: Gulp.

Advisor: Did you say, "Gulp"?

Client: Or words to that effect.

Advisor: Hey, that's nothing. You should have seen 1973-74, when Vietnam was Vietnam, Nixon was getting chased, and the price of oil was doubling every time you turned around. You want to talk about fear...

Client: Do I dare ask where the Dow was then?

Advisor: Round numbers, 600.

Client: I'm getting off the phone now.

Advisor: Wait! Do you understand that I don't know where, how, or when this apocalypse *du jour* is going to end, or where the market will turn? That I'm not telling you it can't go lower?

Client: Yes, but you're also telling me I don't need to worry about it – and that if I do elect to keep worrying, I'm liable to make a really big mistake.

Advisor: That, and one other thing: do you have any additional capital you might be able to invest, while most people around you are still acting on their fears?

The apocalypse *du jour* is like the crosstown bus: if you miss this one, just wait. There'll be another one along in about fifteen minutes. And people will get terrified – in exactly the same way – all over again.

But next time, I hope you'll be ready. Remember: argue never. Reason rarely, and stop as soon as you can. **Empathize always.**

– *NMI*, January 2001

THE LAW OF THE SOGGY POTATO CHIP

Twenty-five years ago, when my two daughters were very young, I heard a famous child psychologist postulate The Law of the Soggy Potato Chip.

He said that a child, not having access to fresh potato chips, will eat soggy potato chips if that's all he can get. And if he can't get real affection and healthy boundaries from his parents, he'll whine and nag and break stuff in order to get exhausted, frustrated feedback from them. Because a small child lives for parental feedback.

I thought of this again the other day when an advisor called me with a question – to which, it turned out, he already knew my answer. (One of the antic joys of being me is getting calls and e-mails from people who say they've read my stuff and love my philosophy – and then proceed to ask a question that either ignores it or denies it.)

This chap said he was relatively new in the business, was very much in the book-building stage, and had recently gotten a referral. The prospect, age 53, asked the advisor what he should do. The advisor correctly replied that the prospect ought to build a pool of capital sufficient to support him through a three-decade retirement and then to become a legacy to his children.

The referral said that he didn't think he was going to live that long, and went away.

The advisor asked my advice. I counseled him to try to forget that this nut job ever existed, and get a good night's sleep. The advisor allowed that he'd anticipated my response (then why did he call me, you ask) but wanted to try to, and I quote, "save the relationship" (what relationship, you ask).

OK, says I; how about this. Call the referral and have him come in for a second meeting. If he won't come, you have well and truly disqualified him: he's no prospect. If he does come, sit him down and say that it didn't seem to you that there'd been a meeting of the minds on the first go-round. Accept the responsibility for this (even though it wasn't your fault) and offer to start over again.

Advisor said he didn't think the referral would go for this. Then what, I asked, did he want me to tell him? The garbled answer I got was that the advisor was seeking my permission to just do whatever the prospect wanted him to, because he needed the business. I said (rather gnomically, because the poor, benighted advisor didn't have the background I've just given you), "You want me to tell you it's OK to eat soggy potato chips. But it's not."

Accepting deeply flawed client relationships is the adult version of "If I can't get Mommy to sit me on her lap and kiss me, I'll get her to yell at me, but I gotta get some feedback. And pass the soggy potato chips." It's the moral equivalent of saying, "I don't know how to find – and probably don't deserve – healthy clients who value me as an advisor and as a person." Over time, this becomes a self-fulfilling prophecy: you start believing all the sad things you're telling yourself – about yourself.

I'm not trying to shrink your head. I'm just trying to suggest that all excellence proceeds from the refusal to eat soggy potato chips, based on three ideas.

First is the unshakable belief that you deserve fresh potato chips – that your work is of sufficient quality ultimately to attract the kind of accounts you want. Second is the adult determination to hold out for fresh potato chips – to direct your excellent efforts to finding excellent accounts, rather than accepting a lot of smaller, lower-quality accounts because you "need" the business. Third is simply having the character to prospect enough people so that, in the end, you get all the fresh potato chips you want – and deserve.

– *Financial Advisor*, January 2001

THE UNICORN, THE GRYPHON AND THE SHORT-TERM INVESTOR

One day during the millennial bear market, I made the mistake of turning on the television, to find a well-regarded Wall Street leader being questioned by a journalistic "personality."

The interviewer ritually asked the guest when or where the market would stop going down. With the patience usually displayed by a kind person talking to a child – which, come to think of it, is just what he was – the executive cautioned that no one can reliably call market turning points.

"But then," the journalist pressed him, affecting her very best imitation of a person capable of genuine concern, "what should the short-term investor do?"

Up to that moment, I had thought that I knew all the inane concepts which financial journalism hallucinates for no other purpose than to keep its audience hooked on the crack cocaine of financial journalism. But the concept of "short-term investing" was, if you'll forgive a particularly dreadful play on words, news to me.

Like "jumbo shrimp," "water landing" and "short-sleeve dress shirt," "short-term investing" is an oxymoron. And the short-term investor, like the unicorn and the gryphon, is a mythical animal. He (or she) is a creature of the Great

Electronic Lie that "every second counts," that hair-trig-ger trading capability is a "new era" improvement on pa-tience and discipline. (In the deepest pit of hell, the most exquisite torture inflicted on the Nazi propaganda genius Joseph Goebbels must surely be the knowledge that he just missed television.)

Call it by its rightful name: *all short-term financial focus is speculation.* Nor must speculation be exclusively short-term in nature. If you're buying and selling specific in-vestments—much less moving in and out of markets—based on any anticipation of changes in price as opposed to changes in value, you're a speculator.

There need be no shame in this. The great economist John Maynard Keynes held that long-term investing is "in-tolerably boring" ("In the long run," he famously wrote, "we are all dead") and proudly called himself a speculator. (Of course, Keynes once came within a whisker of going broke trading commodities, but then who hasn't?) Just don't confuse speculation with investing.

Investing is a fundamental commitment of one's core capi-tal to the pursuit of the great goals of life: the education of one's children and grandchildren, an income one cannot outlive in a dignified and independent retirement, a legacy for those one loves and must leave behind in the world.

These are goals (and therefore investing must be a plan) that will play out over decades, and indeed over generations. Journalism's mayfly perspective is no part of the solution, and may be a big part of the problem. Indeed, if "short-term investing" is an oxymoron, "long-term investing" is (or ought to be) a redundancy.

The particular financial storm at sea which journalism decries today will not only fail to affect my children's children's wealth, but that sea itself may in their day have dried up. Thus, as the steward of their capital, I must think not in electronic but in virtually geologic time. That doesn't necessarily make me smart, but it does make me an investor.

Last year, on my 33rd anniversary in the investment profession, I was interviewed by someone who perceptively asked, "Knowing what you know now, what one thing would you have done differently?"

I answered that I'd never have been afflicted with the conceit that I could anticipate market movements. All my real success as both investor and advisor started when I abandoned any market viewpoint, and determined that one need only stay in it to win it.

Go and do likewise.

– *Financial Advisor*, February 2001

AND IF YOU STILL BELIEVE
IN THE EFFICIENT MARKET THEORY,
HE'S GOT A DAM TO SELL YOU

"It is difficult for economic policy to deal with the abrupt-ness of a break in confidence. There may not be a seam-less transition from high to moderate to low confidence on the part of businesses, investors, and consumers. Looking back at recent cyclical episodes, we see that the change in attitudes has often been sudden. In earlier testimony, I likened this process to water backing up against a dam that is finally breached. The torrent carries with it most remnants of certainty and euphoria that built up in ear-lier periods. This unpredictable rending of confidence is one reason that recessions are so difficult to forecast. They may not be just changes in degree from a period of eco-nomic expansion, but a different process engendered by fear. Our economic models have never been particularly successful in capturing a process driven in large part by nonrational behavior."

> – Fed Chairman Alan Greenspan,
> semiannual monetary policy report
> to the Congress, February 13, 2001

Q&A: ESCHEW SECTOR BETS

Q: *Do you have an opinion on specialty funds, for example electronics, financial services, etc.? In the past, I've stuck with large-cap growth, large-cap value, small-cap growth, and so on, and let the manager diversify among the sectors. I am contemplating using specialty funds in my practice and would like your thoughts on if and how to mix them in.*

A: I'm opposed to advisors making sector bets of any kind, and quite strongly opposed to open-end sector mutual funds. You hire managers in broad categories like big-cap growth, small-cap value, etc., to use their own judgment in choosing sectors. Sector funds are, to me, the worst form of managing your managers, then paying a full-boat management fee in return for very narrowly circumscribed stock selection. If you insist on having your client in a particular sector – and I say again: you shouldn't – pick the top two or three stocks in the sector, buy a unit investment trust, or buy an exchange-traded fund.

– *NMI*, February 2001

Q&A: KEEPING THE FAITH

Q: I realize that it is a long-term perspective that should guide us. It is hard to keep the faith in these perilous times. Any pearls to offer?

A: These aren't perilous times; these are glorious times. The U.S. stands at an unprecedented peak of economic power in the world. Our model of democratic capitalism is the one which most of the world is striving to copy. Our productivity is continuing to accelerate. We have budget surpluses and a big tax cut coming. The greatest financial bubble in the history of the world has finally burst, so far with no serious consequences to the rest of the market or the economy. Interest rates are cratering. The right guy – or at least the right philosophy of government – got elected. And huge chunks of the stock market are on sale.

A looming war in the Middle East, a nationwide banking crisis and a **real** recession in 1990-91: *those* were perilous times. Hyperinflation in 1979-80, with $800 gold, 10% unemployment and a 15% prime rate: those were perilous times. A president getting chased, an oil embargo and Vietnam in 1973-74: those were perilous times. Pearl Harbor: America suddenly at war across both oceans, with the smallest standing army in the industrialized world: that was a perilous time.

Do I have any pearls? Try these four, which I invite you to write out in your own hand and recite aloud every hour on the hour. Numbers One and Three are quotes from me (hey, that rhymes) and the other two are as indicated. (1) The ability to distinguish between a temporary decline in the price of your investments and a permanent loss in their value is the first casualty of a bear market. (2) "The only thing we have to fear is fear itself." – FDR. (3) Optimism is the only realism; it's the only world-view that's consistent with the historical record. (4) "If you're not part of the solution, you're part of the problem." – Huey P. Newton.

– *NMI*, March 2001

Q&A: SELECTING MANAGERS

Q: In your books and Master Class®, you talk about creating diversified equity fund portfolios. Do you have any recommendations about how to search out managers in each of your categories (big-cap growth, small-cap value, etc.) who meet your criteria?

A: No; I never did it scientifically, not least of all because I don't think there's any reliable left-brain way to do it. In a diversified equity fund portfolio such as I recommend, what you're looking for is managers passionately committed to their style, be it in or out of favor. The enemy of diversification isn't underperformance, whatever that means, but style drift. So once you know what categories you want, you look for "managers on a mission." I did this eyeball-to-eyeball, not through a screen, or at least not ultimately through a screen.

Finally, as I always do, let me remind you that it doesn't matter. What managers do, both absolutely and relative to each other, pales in importance next to what the investor – guided by his advisor – does. I feel constrained ritually to repeat: financial success isn't driven by investment performance but by investor behavior, and your primary function is that of behavior modifier, not manager handicapper.

– *NMI*, April 2001

Q&A: THE CLIENT WHO REFUSES
TO UNDERSTAND FEES

Q: *I'm a big fan of all your work. My question is about portfolio rebalancing. I got a $500,000 IRA rollover 18 months ago. Because he is a "Nervous Nellie," we chose to dollar-cost average the monies over six months. He is also fee-sensitive. We invested in a diversified mix of funds. It's a fee-based account, and he sees the one percent deducted on a quarterly basis. Since the market decline, he wants to know what he's paying me for, noting that I haven't made any changes to his portfolio. I told him that he pays me to act as a behavior modifier, who prevents him from following his – wrong – instincts. I explained that his funds are appropriate given his goals; they have simply performed as their underlying markets have. He conceptually understood this but still questions what I'm doing for my fee. He thinks some minor tinkering was in order. I don't see how I could have done so without a crystal ball, which I don't have. When do you think portfolio rebalancing is warranted?*

A: Forgive me, but your inquiry isn't about rebalancing at all. It's about trying to deal with someone who neither understands nor appreciates the value of your work.

First, to the issue of allowing the client to dollar-cost average with a lump sum because he is, and I quote, a nervous nellie. Your letter is silent on whether you advised against this, so I can't tell how much blame attaches to him and how much to you. However, if you were "a big fan of all my work" you'd have remembered from page 243 of *The New Financial Advisor* and pps. 122-23 of *Simple Wealth, Inevitable Wealth* that DCA with a lump sum is a very big no-no.

Second, there's no such thing as a "fee-sensitive" client. There are clients who see the value of a fee-based advisor (behavioral help, objectivity, low turnover, etc.) and those who don't. Yours doesn't, and I believe never will. You seem to be in denial about this. The sentence, "He conceptually understands this but still questions what I'm doing for my fee" is a contradiction.

You don't get paid for market timing (the euphemism for which, in your note, is rebalancing) not least of all because you can't do it. You cannot and should not have been expected to tweak this portfolio because of, or especially in anticipation of, gyrations in the markets. The fact that your client thinks you should means he either doesn't understand or has emotionally rejected everything you've told him.

My recommendation is to simply fire the client, on the perfectly logical grounds that he seems unable to understand or to buy into what you do and how you charge for it.

If that's too radical, give him *Simple Wealth, Inevitable Wealth*, and let *me* explain to him how you earn your fee. If he only reads Chapter One, he should get it. Hell, if he only reads the last paragraph on page 27, he should get it.

If he doesn't, *then* fire him.

– *NMI*, May 2001

Q&A: THE CLIENT WHO ISN'T LISTENING

Q: *I have a client who invested with a growth manager in March 2000 (right about the top) as part of a carefully balanced equity diversification strategy. She is now angry about this growth manager being down. We reviewed at the time that this was an aggressive manager, and she was OK with that. Since then, she is down 27% annualized – while her benchmark Nasdaq index is down 54%. My reassurances about how we're diversified and that this is a much longer-term process than just one year seem to be falling on deaf ears. The fact that her manager is handily outperforming the benchmark doesn't seem to be doing any good, and she now talks about going entirely to cash until "things settle down." Your thoughts?*

A: The problem, I suspect, is not that her growth account went down a lot. That was just the proximate cause of the problem surfacing (indeed, boiling over). The problem is that the investor never bought into the plan, which is usually – though not always – a way of saying she didn't buy into you.

At any rate, I think the damage is done, and that – if it makes you feel any better – most of it had been done before you arrived on the scene. I doubt that the account can be saved, and don't think you want to save it. Your client had, and continues to have, expectations that aren't reasonable, and she isn't listening.

I cite three telltale symptoms. (1) If she's not prepared to see even a part of her equity portfolio go down 30% – much less the whole portfolio – then she can't be in equities, and never could. Either somebody neglected to tell her that 30% declines come along as often as the crosstown bus, or she didn't hear you. (2) If she can't accept that a growth manager who's down half as much as the Nasdaq is doing a superb and even brilliant job, she's not listening. (3) If she'd even think of going all to cash, she doesn't understand long-term investing, nor the relationship between a well-diversified long-term portfolio and the achievement of her financial goals. Assuming you explained these things to her, we now know she wasn't listening.

I recommend that you sit down with her and a third party – presumably your branch manager, or whoever your immediate supervisor is – and see if you can get the plan/portfolio back on track. If you can't, I strongly suggest you resign the account, and the sooner the better. Because let this market take another leg down, and you're going to be in arbitration with this person.

There's something valuable to be learned from every intense client interaction – even one as unpleasant as this – and I urge you to go over this whole situation to see if you can figure out what it is. I suspect that you'll find that you were relying on a consummately rational portfolio strategy – which yours clearly is – to overcome the essential irrationality of the person you were dealing with – and with whom you probably always had difficulty communicating.

This never works.

Now, having learned a good lesson, I recommend that you withdraw from the situation as gracefully as you can.

– *NMI*, June 2001

Q&A: THE RETURN OF THE
FAMILY FINANCIAL OFFICE

Q: *What is your opinion regarding the future of solo advisors? Are the big firms really going to dominate or will I be forced to form a partnership or merge with others?*

A: Neither the big firms nor anybody else is ever going to "dominate" financial services at the retail level; it isn't a business that lends itself to "dominance," although it will clearly continue to consolidate.

What *is* true is that we're heading back to the future: toward holistic, seamless financial planning done under one roof – or under a very few networked/allied roofs. We're going, in other words, back to the pre-Glass-Steagall paradigm of the family financial office, now to be shared by 200-300 affluent families/households per advisor. All of a family's affairs may not necessarily be handled *in* that office but I think they'll tend to be handled *through* that office.

I don't know that this is a threat to solo practitioners *per se*, but it surely is a threat to narrowly focused practices (*just* asset management or *just* insurance, for example). So if you only wanted to be a CIMC, you might want to start networking formally with, if not actually merging practices with, a CLU, a CFP and a CPA. Such practices have the potential to be very powerful in the world as I see it developing.

Financial advisory is an intensely relationship-oriented, highly personal kind of service. As such it is neither terribly fee-sensitive nor readily commoditized – which are, of course, two ways of saying the same thing. Don't worry too much about alleged industry megatrends. Serve your 200-300 families superbly well, and you'll prosper no matter what the competitive environment.

– *NMI*, June 2001

Q&A: MURRAY'S FIRST AND SECOND LAWS OF THE MADNESS OF INVESTMENT COMMITTEES

Q: *I recently made a proposal for managing money for a church committee – all members were great except for one attorney who ranted about fees, expenses, etc. and proposed the group pick its own funds. I framed the issue as one of help vs. no help, but this attorney was totally unmoved and kept trying to argue with me. I am not taking the $250,000 account. Isn't it as important that all members trust me as it would be if it were a one-on-one relationship? Any advice?*

A: One of the enduring myths of our profession is that the institutional sales process is rational in a way that dealing with individual investors is not. Each of us has to learn the hard way two important ideas. (1) The 12 smartest people in town, formed into an institutional investment committee, become the single dumbest person in town. (2) A committee is only as rational as its craziest member.

My advice would have been to withdraw your proposal and excuse yourself – with exquisite courtesy – as soon as it became clear that this guy wasn't going to stop beating you up. Now, no matter what anyone says to you, you must refuse to take the account while this nut remains on the committee. And yes, all the members have to trust you, but even more than that: the committee's relationship to you, like any client's, must be premised on their conviction that you add value in excess of your cost, *however that value may be denominated.*

Now, go find a nice, sane, functional human family that (a) has $250,000 and (b) needs and wants your good help.

– *NMI*, July 2001

Q&A: PROSPECTING CONSISTENCY

Q: *I know from* TNFA *your belief that prospecting has to be consistent. Since going independent, and with nobody looking over my shoulder, I've found myself tending to back-slide on my needs to prospect, and to meet with clients, one-on-one. I've always been well-disciplined, but now that I'm on my own, it's easy to let my day fill up with everything but the critical things that I know I should be doing. Particularly now with portfolios in the red, I'm experiencing a lot of call reluctance. How would you advise me?*

A: By making three observations. (1) First and foremost – although I can't prove it – you're not "on your own." God is watching you. If you don't believe that, at least please believe that your conscience is watching you. And when it sees you avoiding what you know you should be doing, you weaken it. (2) It is, indeed, seductively easy to backslide...unless you're truly committed to excellence, in which case it's impossible: you simply won't allow yourself to do it. If you need some externally enforced discipline, try one of Aaron Hemsley's (www.aaronhemsley.com) "trap contracts": write a series of checks for $50 to the organization you hate most in the world, and mail one for every prospecting/client contact behavior you were supposed to perform each day and didn't. (3) I completely fail to understand how anyone who's read, and claims to admire, *TNFA* could use a phrase like "in the red," or be daunted by a down market. Substitute the phrase "on sale" instead, and let no one be safe from your enthusiasm for sale prices. All great advisors – not some, not most, **all** – thrive on, and are totally energized by, bear markets. Worry that this one will end before you get back on your horse.

Please read *TNFA* again, slowly and carefully, cover to cover. My overall concern is that you may have unconsciously edited out of your memory the parts you weren't ready to deal with. (There's a lot of that going around.) And lighten up. The beginning of any solution is the admission – and yours is laudably candid – that you have a problem. You'll be fine.

– *NMI*, July 2001

Q&A: RESISTING THE "HEROIC" IMPULSE

Q: *I have a question regarding the use of hedge funds as an asset class. Is there a place for a hedge component in a well-diversified stock fund portfolio? My accounts are 100% equities (large-cap value, large-cap growth, and international) with a high degree of diversification. Should I consider putting 10% of my clients' portfolios in an actively managed fund that invests in hedge funds? In the long term, would it increase return and reduce volatility? Or could it maintain the return while reducing short-term volatility?*

A: I think there's something in the best of us whereby, when we have finally achieved enough wisdom to craft superbly diversified equity portfolios for our clients and now need only leave them alone to do their glorious work, we find ourselves unable to leave them alone. Your inquiry is, I believe, prompted by this impulse.

Let me make a few general observations, in no particular order of importance. (1) Hedge funds are not an asset class; they're a management style — or rather, a mixed bag of highly idiosyncratic management styles, as wildly disparate as hedge fund managers themselves. (2) Hedging is a high-reward, high-risk management style; neither it nor any management style can provide meaningfully higher long-term returns without concomitantly increased risk. The notion that a hedge fund, much less a whole basket of hedge funds, could provide meaningful melioration of short-term volatility is (a) an absurdity on its face and (b) irrelevant, as all short-term issues are irrelevant. (3) The cost structure of a fund of hedge funds – involving two layers of asset management fees plus your compensation (however it may be buried) – could not fail to destroy the ultimately illusory incremental return. (4) The fundamental notion that changing the character of 10% of your portfolios would meaningfully alter their long-term returns or volatility is mathematically improbable in the extreme.

The fundamental issue here, if you will permit me to say so, isn't hedging at all, but the deep need in us to try to be heroes for our clients. (However misguided, this is always laudable.) I would invite you to snap out of it, and observe (a) that your clients don't need you to be a hero; they need you to help them achieve their goals, which you are so clearly doing, and (b) that you are already a hero for the ages, because you already have your clients' long-term capital entirely in equities, which not one advisor in a hundred ever achieves.

– *NMI*, July 2001

Q&A: IN REPORTING TO CLIENTS, LESS IS MORE

Q: *How do you keep clients focused on the long term while at the same time providing ongoing communication? When I call my clients on a regular basis, the conversation always comes back to "the market" and current conditions. What should I discuss when I call my clients monthly? What type of written communication should I send to clients, and how often should I send it?*

A: Without an agenda – without a purpose for the call – a monthly call can't help but degenerate into navel-gazing about "the market." The larger issue, I think, is how well you've trained your clients to ignore the market – or at least not to talk to you about it, because they know you don't pay any attention to it. With respect, it doesn't sound as if you're there yet. One way to head off this discussion, if you insist on making monthly calls, is to ask people if they have any more money to invest before the sale ends. Bottom line: don't make regular calls just to keep in touch. Have an agenda for each series of calls: financial planning, long-term care insurance (which everyone needs and no one has), whatever. Have an agenda that shows you to be proactive and planning-oriented.

As for written reports, annually is plenty often enough. And the focus of the report shouldn't be a comparison of "performance." It should be an analysis of how far the clients' long-term plan has come in the last year, and the goals of the plan for the next year – including how much more they need to invest over the next 12 months, and in what.

If you insist on saying anything even marginally related to the current market, you may wish to consider the very best four words of advice I've ever gotten about the market: **Don't fight the Fed**.

– *NMI*, September 2001

SEPTEMBER 11, 2001
FOUR READINGS

(When the stock market re-opened in a panic-driven free fall on Monday, September 17, 2001, I posted an essay on my website, "This Time Isn't Different." I believed that the galvanic effect on America of the terrorist atrocities of September 11 meant that, like Pearl Harbor, the event itself would be the turning point.

A month or so later, I attempted to explore the Pearl Harbor analogy further in a newsletter piece, "A Moment Of Maximum Opportunity." In one very important sense it was wrong, in that I was more sanguine about the stock market than was justified by subsequent events. And we were in a recession even before September 11, though no one could be sure of it at the time. But the piece still stands up, I think, in suggesting that both Pearl Harbor and September 11 were a beginning rather than an end.

Two other, more personal essays, "What Would Mom And Dad Have Guessed?" and "I Feel Like I Owe It To Someone," appeared in the newsletter in later months.)

THIS TIME ISN'T DIFFERENT

Sir John Templeton is supposed to have said that the four most dangerous words in investing are "this time is different." Nothing directly comparable to September 11 and its aftermath has ever happened in America, and so it would be all too easy for us – advisor and investor alike – to surrender to this four-word synthesis.

Harry Truman said that the only thing new in the world is the history you don't know. But at a moment like this, when all seems different in terrible and threatening ways, we may conclude that the real danger to us and our clients is in the history we choose to ignore.

All real crisis is new and different in some respects. Pearl Harbor surely appeared at the time to be something utterly without precedent in the American experience. So did the Cuban missile crisis, Vietnam, the Cambodian incursion and the killings at Kent State, the confluence of OPEC and Watergate, stagflation, the October 1987 stock market event, and even Long-Term Capital Management.

If one sees the current situation as unique, or entirely new – if one regards it somehow as a break with history – there will be a terrible temptation to make The Big Mistake. But would anyone, given another chance, sell out of his investments in the days after December 7, 1941? And was the real challenge to America then not infinitely greater than it is now?

The one truly unprecedented thing in human history, I think, is the success of the United States – its institutions, its society, its economy and its markets. This success is not separable from the crises we have encountered; it is, rather, a fabric woven out of those challenges, and out of our particular genius for mastering them.

If history is any guide, you don't "protect" long-term investment capital by taking it out of the equity market, but by leaving it in, and thereby keeping it exposed to the healing power of time – to the resilience of the American economy, and of the markets which reflect it.

Investment decisions based on long-term and even multi-generational financial goals usually turn out to be right, while current events-driven speculation on "what the market might do next" is usually wrong, and many people's lifetime plans never recover from it.

We advisors can neither control nor be responsible for human nature, and a predilection to pessimism will consume some of our clients no matter what we say. But consider asking, "If the World Trade Center were still standing, would you sell today?" If the answer is no, people are admitting that they're panicking out of their long-term investments in a market that's already down 32%. Surely that's a decision they're going to regret, and sooner than later.

At extraordinary moments like this, when our clients are

looking to us for guidance, we have a fairly simple choice: we can either be part of the solution, or we will surely be part of the problem. And the essential gift we have to offer our clients is not prediction, but perspective. For, as Churchill said, the further we look back, the further we may see ahead.

This time isn't different.

– *NMI*, October 2001

A MOMENT OF MAXIMUM OPPORTUNITY

Against all reason and probability, the attack was supremely successful – much more so than its planners could ever have dared to hope. The surprise was total, the destruction – of ships, planes and men – utterly devastating. Eighteen warships, including eight battleships, were sunk or seriously damaged.

At about 11 p.m. Washington time that night – Sunday, December 7, 1941 – Treasury secretary Morgenthau held an emergency briefing for his senior staff. Speaking from depths of shock and exhaustion, he expressed the universal consensus view of the day's events: "It is past unexplainable...it is much worse than anyone realizes...the whole fleet in one place...they will never be able to explain it..."

The next morning, the stock market collapsed.

From March 24, 2000 through Monday, September 10, 2001, about one in three dollars of American stock market capitalization disappeared, as the greatest financial bubble in the history of the world – tech/telecom mania in general, and the dot.com dance of death in particular – came to its inevitable, ignominious end.

Of course, the real destruction in real people's portfolios was often an order of magnitude greater than one third, because they'd underdiversified into the "new era" *du jour*. Just as in 1973-74 – when the broad market went down 48% but the Nifty Fifty growth stocks in the mob's portfolio lost upwards of twice as much – this time wasn't different. *It never is.*

We don't know for sure whether, by September 10, the U.S. economy had actually tipped into recession or not. And that, too, has its precedent: in the late spring of 1990, the economy – staggered by the worst banking crisis since the '30s, the liquidation of the S&L system and a rising tide of corporate downsizing – either had or had not slipped into recession. When Saddam's tanks rolled into Kuwait, the point became moot – exactly as it would on September 11, 2001.

But the very fact that we're not sure if we were in recession on September 10 is itself a species of miracle. Take a moment, if you will, to marvel at the depth, diversity and resilience of an economy that could absorb the unwinding of the greatest financial mania in history – with all the horrific misallocation of resources that such a bubble entails – and merely go flat to barely negative. For, like Sherlock Holmes's dog that didn't bark in the night, this is a most important clue.

But almost immediately, as the shock of December 7 began to give way to a newfound and vigorous determination, a different view took shape. Secretary Morgenthau had been

*wrong; **everyone** had been wrong. The situation was **not** worse than anyone realized, because in fact the whole fleet had **not** been in one place. Our aircraft carriers had been out to sea. And the single greatest lesson of the attack on Pearl Harbor was precisely that this new war would be fought between carriers rather than between battleships. Those naval assets which would – sooner than anyone could imagine – prove decisive to the war in the Pacific **were perfectly intact**.*

After September 11, 2001, there could no longer be much doubt of the economy's ability to stage a recession, classically defined: two quarters – most probably 3Q and 4Q01 – of negative GDP growth. (*Editor's note*: In fact, the recession ran from the first through the third quarter.) The virtual cardiac arrest of the travel/tourism/hospitality industry, massive layoffs (perhaps 100,000 jobs lost in New York City alone), retrenchment in financial services, huge insurance losses – the terrorist atrocities may well have completed what the bursting of the tech bubble started. And yet these disasters, in their way, may be akin to the sunken battleships: what's terribly wrong is immediately and rivetingly obvious, but by staring at it we may miss the larger, more important point.

That point – which in the longer run must prove decisive, as did the carriers – is the tidal wave of fiscal and monetary stimulus which is even now engulfing the flames of an event-driven recession.

By almost immediately cutting short-term rates another 100 basis points, and by flooding the crippled financial system with huge injections of liquidity, the Federal Reserve put the full year 2001 in the record books as the setting for the deepest, fastest interest rate reduction in its history. (The previous record rate cuts, culminating in mid-1982, set off the greatest bull market in history...as how could they not?)

Moreover, the proposed $100 billion in post-9/11 fiscal stimulus, added to that of the tax rate reductions due in 2002 and beyond, cannot fail to fuel the eventual recovery of confidence upon which renewed economic expansion is always built. If the timing of this resurgence of confidence cannot be predicted, its inevitability cannot be doubted.

The next thing our military leaders realized was that, in the incredibly target-rich environment that was Pearl Harbor that Sunday morning, the attackers had completely neglected to hit the Navy's state-of-the-art supply and repair facilities: they were undamaged.

Moreover, the very condition that had created the illusion of invulnerability at Pearl – water too shallow for airborne torpedo attack, until the great gambler Yamamoto perfected a way of doing it – meant that our ruined ships sank in only a couple of fathoms. From there, they could be repaired, pumped out and refloated. And they were. Excepting only the battleships Arizona *and* Oklahoma, ***every major warship destroyed at Pearl Harbor got back into the war in 1943 and 1944.***

The combined effect of the end of technology mania and the terrorist atrocities of September 11 was a stock market that fell (as measured by the S&P 500) 37% in 18 months (3/24/00-9/21/01) less one weekend. This is the second deepest and – by a mere 18 days – the third longest bear market of the post-WWII period. Perhaps more to the point, it is the first bear market of even average (roughly 12 months) duration in nearly 20 years. It goes without saying, then, that an entire generation of investors is seeing a real bear market for the first time – a bear market their "new era" gurus had told them couldn't happen anymore.

What is less obvious, but even more important, is that **half the financial advisors licensed in America today entered the profession since the historic bear market lows of October 11, 1990**. What we have here is a classic case of the blind leading the blind.

This creates the perfect situation for the potentially excellent advisor – a moment of maximum opportunity, such as one experiences perhaps only once in a career.

First, the equity investments you recommend in this period will be at or near lows which – like those of 1990, of

1974, and even of the period after Pearl Harbor – will, I'm convinced, be not merely cyclical but historic: you will literally never see some of these prices again as long as you live.

Second, a whole generation of clients is in the process of being orphaned, as the flotsam and jetsam that washed into the advisory profession on the flood tide of the 1990s washes back out again. And even the great mass of marginal advisors who manage to hang on will have irreparably damaged many or most of their client relationships with their new-era "advice," such that those accounts are now in play.

Finally, I believe we have good reason to hope that the events of the last year and a half have driven a stake through the heart of the toxic fiction of do-it-yourself. Nothing more clearly shows the value of advice than the devastation people bring down on themselves when they think they can do without it.

All these windows are gloriously open now. But they will close – sooner than you think they will, and *much* sooner than you want them to.

Six months less one day after Pearl Harbor – as the sun set in the Pacific on June 6, 1942 – virtually all the Japanese carriers which had taken part in the attack lay at the bottom of the ocean. And the great preponderance of the

aviators who had flown off their decks and into history just six months earlier were dead. Beginning in the Coral Sea, and now at Midway, the ability of the Japanese navy to wage offensive war had been utterly destroyed.

Yamamoto – an honorable man who understood America's industrial might and respected its people's greatness – knew that he had missed his chance at Pearl. He risked everything on one more roll of the dice at Midway, and lost. A year more and he himself was dead: having long since broken the Japanese codes, our fighters intercepted his plane and blew it out of the sky.

Pearl Harbor, appearing in its moment the enemy's unalloyed triumph, was instead his death knell. Pearl Harbor, appearing to be the nadir of American power, was instead the turning point of the entire global conflict. That supreme outrage galvanized the energies of the nation, and gave every American, in Gordon W. Prange's words, "a cause he could understand and believe to be worth fighting for."

I was born, almost to the day, halfway between Pearl Harbor and V-J Day. Thus, I have no memory of the war; I know only what I've read, but I've read a fair amount.

I never thought I'd live to see our nation's people, resources and will energized and focused as they were by Pearl Harbor. I was wrong. I never thought I'd live to hear people all across this country say, "We are all New Yorkers." I was wrong. Above all, perhaps, I could never dream that the French newspaper *Le Monde* would ever be moved to write, *"Nous sommes tous Americains."* I was wrong.

As an investor, as an advisor, as an American – for your clients, for your family, for yourself – please, please take a good look around. *It's happening again.* The World Trade Center is this generation's Pearl Harbor. If history is any guide – and it's the only guide I'll ever need, or even want – this moment of maximum uncertainty will show itself to have been the moment of maximum opportunity. And it will do so all too soon.

This time isn't different. And there may not be a moment to lose.

– *NMI*, November 2001

THREE TENTHS OF ONE PERCENT:
WHAT WOULD MOM AND DAD
HAVE GUESSED?

The government recently reported that economic activity in 3Q01, as measured by GDP, contracted by three tenths of one percent. That made me think about my mom and dad.

My father was born in 1909, and my mother in 1913. They were very much of that generation who came to adulthood in the Great Depression, and it informed (if it didn't actually form) the way they looked at the world.

My folks always said that no one would ever forget where they were when they heard about Pearl Harbor, and again when they learned that FDR had died. I didn't know what they meant until about one o'clock on the afternoon of November 22, 1963. And I don't suppose anyone will forget where they were when they heard about what was happening on September 11, 2001.

My parents have been gone a long time – far too long, really: neither of them ever saw the World Trade Center. So I wondered what it would be like if I could tell them about the events of the last couple of years.

Mom and Dad, I'd say, you always remembered the Crash of 1929 – how a whole era just vanished in one terrible day on Wall Street, and how darkness descended for the next dozen years. Well, of the 100 million people in the U.S. that day, only about three million owned stocks, and perhaps 600,000 of them were on margin.

Now, in my time, we've just had an investment bubble that dwarfs the '20s, and everybody – working men and women, blue collar people, retirees – everybody got caught in it. Why, the market was still coming down 18 months after the bubble burst. And like radio stocks in your day, our revolutionary technology companies went down 80% and 90%. People on margin were wiped out.

My folks would say, I think, that that sounded even worse than what they remembered.

Then I'd remind them of the stories they told me about Pearl Harbor, where 2400 sailors and soldiers died in a sneak attack. I'd tell them that, 18 months into my bear market, terrorists crashed huge airplanes into the two tallest buildings in New York, and killed nearly 3000 civilians. That set off a world war against an enemy we couldn't see; the economy went into a seizure, and the stock market crashed all over again.

And then, just for fun, *I'd ask them how much they thought the economy went down in the calendar quarter when all those terrible events came together in an historic, utterly unprecedented cataclysm.*

I've been asking my seminar audiences – industry and

client alike – what they thought my mom and dad would answer. The range of estimates I've gotten so far is 10% to 90%, with most guesses in the 25% to 40% bracket.

If I could tell my folks that the answer is three tenths of one percent, I'm pretty sure they'd think that was some kind of miracle. And I think they'd wonder why so many people alive today think this is the end of the world.

– *NMI*, December 2001

I FEEL LIKE I OWE IT TO SOMEONE

Herman Sandler's and my tenure at Bear Stearns over-lapped only for a couple or three years in the mid-1980s. I never really got to know him, not least of all because he was a bond guy – indeed, one of those bond geniuses whom the Bear has always incubated.

Herman and 65 of his 171 partners, friends and colleagues at Sandler O'Neill & Partners, whose offices were on the 104th floor of the World Trade Center, died on September 11th. He was five months younger than I.

Fortune's January 21, 2002 issue leads with an extraordi-nary cover story about the way in which Sandler O'Neill is battling back, refusing to disappear. I confess, though, that that human and corporate struggle isn't what struck me most about the story.

It was the caption below a picture of Herman's widow and three daughters that got me. "My dad never brought a briefcase home," daughter Jordana says. "My dad believed in having fun."

You see, it wasn't all that long ago that my son Mark caus-tically referred to *my* briefcase as my best friend. Now, my life is my family and my work, and I've always main-tained that I work as hard as I do because I love them – and want for them – as much as I do. But as the "best friend" crack makes clear, there have been times when the alleged beneficiaries of my labor found it (and, if I'm brutally honest, me) a high price to pay. I can fairly say I'm getting better at this – with my family's continued encouragement, and not without their occasional veiled threat – but Jordana Sandler's observation hit me very hard. And, should you feel the need, I give you permission to have it hit you hard, as well.

When Robert Kennedy died, David Crosby wrote a song that was a cry of pain and loss, but also a promise to memorialize RFK's courage in his own life from then on. The song's title was its first line:

> Almost cut my hair.
> It happened just the other day.
> It was gettin' kind of long;
> I could have said it was in my way.
> But I didn't, and I wonder why
> I feel like letting my freak flag fly.
> **I feel like I owe it to someone.**

This may not sound like much. And it may not even be much. But I'm never going to bring my briefcase home again. I feel like I owe it to someone.

– *NMI,* February 2002

ENDOWING CHILDREN VS. SPOILING THEM:
THE GREAT DEBATE
AND THE HIDDEN AGENDA

Now and again – most recently in the last Nick Murray Master Class® – an advisor will get seriously on my case about my contention that there is no rational argument for a long-term investment strategy based preponderantly if not solely on bonds.

The challenge most often comes from someone with a client to whom bonds would provide, and I quote, "more income than they'll ever need." My response is that this contention is either stupid or evil, and quite possibly both.

It's stupid when "more income than they'll ever need" turns out merely to mean "much more income than they need now and *can ever imagine needing*." Maybe "stupid" is too harsh a description of this psychology (and then again, maybe it isn't). Perhaps it should just be regarded as a failure of imagination.

A nice 60-year-old couple – with a joint life expectancy of 30 years – sells their business for eight million dollars after taxes. They can get, from an intelligently laddered portfolio of tax-free municipal bonds, $400,000 a year, let's say. And they can't imagine themselves spending $200,000 a year, particularly in excess of Social Security. So why take, and I quote again, "the risk of the stock market"?

I'll tell you why. Because at trendline inflation, their $200,000 living costs will be pushing $600,000 30 years from now. Moreover, these good folks (or at least the survivor) will be in the throes of incurring half their total lifetime medical expenditures during the last five years of life. (And if you believe *any* Western government will be able to provide comprehensive health care in 30 years, given baby boomer demographics, you'll believe anything.)

On the other hand, let's say this nice couple has not eight but $20 million from the sale of the business – and still only $200,000 of core living costs. Given normal inflation, they actually may get "more income than they'll ever need" from those municipal bonds. So for them, bonds aren't necessarily stupid. Instead, assuming the couple has children and grandchildren, bonds are certainly evil. Because, through bonds, these folks are going to steal their heirs' patrimony.

In 30 years, with both parents gone, the heirs will get the $20 million bond portfolio, and pay, let's say, half in estate taxes. That will leave $10 million – *or less than $3.5 million in then-current purchasing power.* Think of it: more than an 80% loss (through inflation and taxes) of the purchasing power of the $20 million – so the parents could feel "safe." That's just...*evil.*

Faced with this incontrovertible argument, advisors trying to justify their own weakness in accepting big bond accounts (because, of course, that's all they're doing) fall back on the *Millionaire Next Door*/Warren Buffett defense: endowing one's children will spoil them.

Please note that no advisor who advances this argument really believes it. Money doesn't spoil kids; *parents* spoil kids. (And they don't need money to do it, either; I see poor people raising rotten kids every day, and so do you.) So because their argument is so counterintuitive – and because they so desperately need it to salve their consciences – advisors vehemently insist that Tom Stanley and Bill Danko, authors of *TMND*, back them up with scientific findings. And they cite Buffett's long and implacable opposition to bequeathing any significant part of his great wealth to his children as further support for their insupportable position.

The only problem is that Stanley and Danko aren't the least little bit anti-inheritance, and that Buffett, in his relationships with his children, has, for most of their lives, behaved with surpassing strangeness.

What Stanley and Danko oppose – and rightly so – is giving adult children cash gifts which are "earmarked for consumption and the propping up of a certain lifestyle." Their research shows just what you'd expect: that people who are given more consumption-oriented cash accomplish (and accumulate) less in life than do people who have to make their own way.

Stanley and Danko aren't against bequeathing wealth;

they're against *people needing their parents' money*. One thing with the other got nothing to do, as an elderly client of mine from the Lower East Side always said. "Economic outpatient care," as the authors call it, is bad. Leaving real wealth to people who are economically self-sufficient isn't just OK by them: it's the desired end, the truly American way.

Buffett is a different, and very special, case. The product of a terrifyingly dysfunctional mother, he has always had (at least until recent years, when he seems to have softened considerably) very odd relationships with his kids. He has at times stood by and let them sell their Berkshire Hathaway stock, knowing that they didn't realize they could borrow against it – and not telling them. One can't help feeling (especially after reading Roger Lowenstein's biography) that his strident disavowal of leaving his kids any real money has been a means not to empower but to deny them. Indeed, to the end of her life, Katharine Graham – who loved Buffett, and relied on him absolutely – said that this issue was the only serious argument they'd ever had.

When all is said and done, I think advisors who use Stanley/Danko/Buffett to (however indirectly) defend bonds are a lot like those who used Harry Dent to advance the crackpot theory that there couldn't be a bear market until 2009, or whenever. That is, they haven't really studied the work they're citing to give their meretricious arguments some illusory intellectual standing.

Because if they had, they'd have found either that their source wasn't saying what they thought it said – or that it was, but indefensibly.

– NMI, October 2001

Q&A: EXPLAINING FEES

Q: *One side of the argument of fees vs. commissions that I have never heard discussed is what is ultimately best for the client. I do quite a bit of business in "A" shares. Like most advisors, I am intrigued by fee-based business, but I simply cannot make the numbers work. When I drop the load and add the fee, my compensation rises dramatically, while the appreciation of my clients' accounts drops by the same proportion. How is this best for the client? I would appreciate your thoughts.*

A: Yours is an important question – actually several important questions. I'm going to respond, as a passionate believer in – and advocate of – fee-based business. But I'd have you understand that I'm neither trying to "sell" you on fees, or off "A" shares. One is not "right" and the other "wrong." They are both ethical and honorable approaches to the practice of retail financial/investment advice.

All of that said, I think your suspicion of fees and your strong belief in "A" shares is clouding your judgment, to the point where your premises and your math are at least suspect. I'd like to separate those issues, and get them out of the way, before stating my case for fees.

To begin with, you seem to be equating "best for the client" with "cheapest," but you don't really mean that. If you did, you wouldn't charge anything. You know, as do we all, that some compensation to the advisor is fair.

Where we differ, as you'll see, is in our concepts of fairness.

Second, I can't follow your math. When you apply a one percent fee (or a "C" share arrangement) to an initial investment, rather than an "A" share, it's the advisor's compensation which drops dramatically, and the investor's return which rises. The crossover, on a present value basis – the point where a one percent fee costs more than an "A" share – doesn't come for about seven years, if my math is holding up. (If *this* is what you meant, I agree with you, but I don't think it is. I took you to be saying that fees immediately ding the client to the advisor's benefit, which is counterintuitive.)

Those issues aside, we return to the essential issue, which to me is fairness. I never had an "A" share practice, would not have one now if I went back into retail advisory, and would counsel anyone entering the field today not to have one. The reason is that I don't believe "A" shares are fair to the quality advisor.

As you know, I believe the essence of good investment advice is behavioral: talking people – again and again, over many years – out of making The Big Mistake. The idea that a one-time commission of some percentage of the initial investment (which, with the proper behavioral advice, will multiply through the years) adequately compensates the advisor is not one that I can accept.

A fee gives the advisor a direct and very real economic interest in the outcome of his advice, for good or ill. It also – and I think this is critical – fairly compensates the advisor for telling the client to do nothing – when, as it almost always is, nothing is the right thing for the client to do.

In my book *The New Financial Advisor*, I pose this question to the prospects, concerning a one percent fee:

"Does it seem probable to you that, with all the resources of my firm behind me, I will:

"(a) cause your long-term investment return to be at least one percent per year more than you might obtain on your own, *and / or*

"(b) save you at least one percent per year in the cost of mistakes I might be able to help you not make, *and / or*

"(c) save you at least the equivalent of one percent per year in time, energy, worry and/or record-keeping?"

Please note that no one of those three services has to be worth one percent to the prospects all by itself. The question carefully – and quite correctly – asks if the prospects think that *any combination* of those three great gifts to a family's financial and emotional well-being would, in all probability, be worth more than our one percent annual fee.

My belief is that the answer is unequivocally yes.

– *NMI*, October 2001

Q&A: THE FATAL ATTRACTION OF ONE'S OWN COMPANY'S STOCK

Q: *A middle-aged client of mine has been offered a low interest loan to buy the common stock of his employer, a blue chip company. The client feels strongly about proceeding with the stock purchase, but I'm concerned that the company stock would represent more than 30% of his investment portfolio. How should I counsel him?*

A: I applaud your concern, and believe it well-founded. Getting underdiversified in a stock to which one may emotionally be up too close is a dangerous business. Knowing nothing else about the client's circumstances, I would just make the general observation that 30% is borderline, not insignificant and not egregiously underdiversified. I think the greatest service you could do the client would be to sit down and do a "what if" disaster scenario, in which you estimate the extent of the damage to the client's lifetime plan if this investment were to become worthless and he still had to pay back his loan.

– *NMI*, November 2001

I HEAR YOUR QUESTION.
NOW, WHAT ARE YOU REALLY ASKING ME?

Any time the market tanks, there's suddenly a devil theory or two abroad in the land, affording people an intellectual excuse for their emotional pessimism.

The two pick hits of the week that I hear most often these days are, in no particular order: (1) This is Japan; it doesn't matter how much interest rates get cut; they've been zero in Japan for years and that economy is still moribund; they and we are in a classic 1930s-style Keynesian "liquidity trap." (2) We're in for several years of substandard equity returns during which an investor will do as well (or better) in bonds.

The first of these two theories is dumb; the second is just counterintuitive, and/or too vague to give the long-term investor any way to strategize around it. But none of that is my point.

The facts are never the fundamental issue in a discussion of the apocalypse *du jour,* as far as a career advisor is concerned. Of far greater importance is the client's anxiety – his unfocused dread – and what potential damage it's in danger of doing, not just to the portfolio but to the relationship.

What the client is looking for here is an excuse to get out of equities. And he will seize on that excuse in either of its two possible forms. First, and the preferred method, is for the advisor to mount an unconvincing (to the client) defense of staying invested given the stated "problem." Second – and they aren't mutually exclusive – is for the advisor to get embroiled in an argument with the client, allowing the investor to get so mad he just lashes out and orders the advisor to sell.

So the biggest mistake the advisor could make is to do exactly what we were all trained to do: "answer the objection." Instead, you'll want to follow *all three* of these behavioral rules. (1) Don't engage directly with the stated issue. (2) Don't accept a burden of proof. (3) Don't argue. Let's see how this might work in practice.

Client: Many experts are saying our economy could be doing what Japan's is, so our stock market could be down in the dumps for years.

Advisor: None of those experts must have gone anywhere near a car dealership lately.

Client: Huh?

Advisor: Sorry. I was just being semi-flippant. Please help me understand your concerns.

Client: I'm worried that what happened in Japan might happen here.

Advisor: It might, I guess, in the sense that anything's possible. But if we worried about everything that's possible, we'd never get out of bed in the morning. The best advice I can give you is: try to stay focused on what's probable in the long run. And it doesn't seem probable that the U.S. will end up in the kind of fix Japan is in.

Client: Why not?

Advisor: Just in the interest of time, because the dissimilarities between our economy and Japan's are so numerous, could I just ask you to give me one similarity that's got you concerned?

Client: Well, as I understand it, they've long since cut interest rates all the way to zero, and the economy's still dead in the water.

Advisor: Dead as ever it's been these dozen years.

Client: Exactly. And we've had all these Fed interest rate cuts, and our economy shows no sign of turning around. And we're getting down toward zero.

Advisor: Now I'm starting to see where you think the parallel might be. Let me just ask you: what do you think is supposed to happen when you get massive interest rate cuts?

Client: Huh? Well...I guess people are supposed to go out and buy stuff...with borrowed money. And that gets the economy going again. I mean, that's right, isn't it?

Advisor: Right as rain. And that's exactly what didn't happen in Japan. At least not yet.

Client: My very point. So why couldn't it happen here?

Advisor: Again, I can think of a lot of reasons it couldn't, or at least wouldn't. But the important thing, I think, is to realize that it didn't.

Client: Now you've completely lost me.

Advisor: Did you see what car sales did in October?

Client: Yeah. They went through the roof, because the car makers cut the interest rate to zero...gulp.

Advisor: What was the last thing you said?

Client: Gulp, or words to that effect. Hey, how could I have missed that? This is America, for crying out loud. You cut car loan rates to zero...

Advisor: Or you let people pull equity out of their homes at the lowest mortgage rates in 30 years...

Client: And people will respond to that!

Advisor: Well, Americans will.

Client: So what's all this noise about Japan?

Advisor: I don't know; you brought it up.

Gentle reader, there isn't a scintilla of similarity between the U.S. economy and Japan's. There wasn't when the Nikkei was pushing 40,000 and the Dow Jones Industrials were still south of 3,000. And there isn't now. They didn't have a post-war baby boom, so they haven't got the huge generation of consumers and retirement savers we do. They're in deflation and have been for years, so you get paid to hold cash in your mattress – *very* bad for an economy. Their banking system is rotten to the core: if they marked all their bad loans to the market, the whole system would be (and, in truth, is) insolvent. And, oh yes, after a dozen years of economic malaise, their unemployment rate is still no higher than ours is. They don't let people go; they don't practice the creative destruction so necessary to clear away the wreckage of an outmoded economic model in order to start fresh.

Now, do you really want to argue all that? And maybe *still* come up empty, because the client's really just having a panic attack?

The other bogeyman of the hour – although I think advisors are much more worked up about this than real clients are, which is often the case – is the notion of an impending period when bond and stocks returns are about the same.

In part, this is just the extrapolation fallacy, wearing the emperor's new (intellectual) clothes. When returns have been high, people instinctively believe that returns will continue to be high. When they've been low, as in the last couple of years…well, you know.

Bill Gross, the highly regarded bond fund manager, has advanced the theory that, for some unspecified number of years, bond and stock returns could both be about five percent per year. He calls this relationship "dysfunctional"; I call it counterintuitive. In any event, (a) I pray heaven it's true, and (b) I'm not going to argue about it. Here's how:

Client: I just saw a very smart guy on CNBC, saying stock and bond returns were going to both be around five percent for years.

Advisor: Why?

Client: Huh?

Advisor: Well, I mean, they don't usually do that. And never have done it for any significant length of time, far as I know. Doesn't mean it couldn't happen, of course, but why did the fellow say it would?

Client: I thought I was supposed to be the one who asked the questions.

Advisor: OK, good. Go ahead and ask me one.

Client: What do you think of the theory that stock and bond returns are going to be about the same for a number of years?

Advisor: I would love for it to be true. So should you, I think. Doesn't seem likely. Wouldn't change anything I do. [Silence]

Client: But if you could get the same returns from bonds...

Advisor: Yes?

Client: ...wouldn't it make sense to switch into bonds?

Advisor: And switch back...when, exactly? Would the same guy tell us when this weird, wonderful period was about to be over?

Client: I see your point, I guess, but why do you keep talking as though this would be a good thing for people in equities?

Advisor: Well, in the cases of you and me, because we're accumulators. I just turned 58, and my last child graduates college in May. I've got, I hope, the next several years to do some serious buying. I'd love to believe that the market would just lie there for a while and let me accumulate shares at anything near these prices. You're a bit younger than I – who isn't, these days – so I should think you'd be pretty happy, too.

Client: But if you could get the same five percent return with no risk...?

Advisor: Who said there's no risk? What if the guy's wrong?

Client: Well...is he?

Advisor: Couldn't tell you. But I don't think an efficient market would accept five percent from stocks and bonds for very long. It'd bid up bonds to higher prices – and lower yields. Least I think it would. Lower yields – lower interest rates, that is – would turn into higher earnings growth and higher stock prices, at some point. And I wouldn't know when that point was coming – wouldn't know when to switch back, in other words. To make this work, you'd have to be right twice, if you see what I mean.

Client: So it'd make the most sense to just stay with equities, and keep pecking away during a period of lower returns…

Advisor: If indeed we were in one.

Client: …even if we were in one…because…because why, again?

Advisor: Well, because when equities started to play catch-up – when they went back up to their normal returns – you'd have laid in many, many barrels of low-priced shares while the bond buyer was off chasing the illusion of "safety."

Client: So why was I alarmed when the guy said this?

Advisor: I have to confess, I didn't understand that either.

Client: Would you please forget we had this conversation?

Advisor: What conversation?

Give most investors a new, "lower" (than what? a bubble?) long-term economic growth rate of two percent to three percent. Give 'em a productivity growth rate which, after the obvious one-time downward adjustment attendant upon increased security/systems redundancy, keeps any kind of pace with technological change. And they'll be very happy they stayed in equities – sooner than later. But again: *do you want to argue that?*

Stay confident. Stay loose, friendly, consultative and – above all – non-argumentative. And all good things will come to you.

– *NMI*, December 2001

A CAUTIONARY NOTE ABOUT
THE WALL STREET WORLD VIEW *DU JOUR*
(WHETHER IT'S *THE GREAT DEPRESSION OF 1990*
OR *THE ROARING 2000'S*)

"One should always be suspicious about methodological protestations from those who deal in markets, whether central bankers or pit traders. They understand the intellectual arguments and can brilliantly expound their methodology of the moment. But over time they tend to pick and choose among methodologies as their mood changes; they want the explanation that gives them the result their instinct says they should reach."

— Robert Bartley, *The Seven Fat Years*

Q&A: FACING PORTFOLIO MISTAKES

Q: *Because I had many of my clients underdiversified, some have lost over 50% of their portfolios. Although I'd like to stick my head in the sand and pretend it never happened, I have been calling these clients and telling them we must learn from the past and become diversified. What words or phrases would you use in this kind of discussion?*

A: I don't think there's any word, combination of words, or technique that would change the experience of what you have to say to your clients, either for you or for them. You made one of the all-time classic, invariably fatal mistakes – underdiversification – in a good, or at least goodhearted, cause: trying to get them superior "performance." Now you and they know a great truth, and this is a mistake you never have to make again. Look in your heart, and find out (by writing out) your own best way to tell them this. Start with the realization and conviction that the right time to redress underdiversification is always (and only) now.

– *NMI*, December 2001

Q&A: DISINFLATION ISN'T DEFLATION

Q: *All your equity investment philosophy is based on the idea of persistent, grinding (if low-level) inflation. But, since 2001, we've been getting whiffs of deflation. When would you be willing to re-examine your approach in light of deflationary pressures?*

A: The day the U.S. Postal Service lowers the price of a first-class postage stamp. And not a moment sooner.

– *NMI*, January 2002

STOP MANAGING MONEY

In my book *The New Financial Advisor*, I say that 95% of one's total lifetime investment return results from one's adherence (or failure to adhere) to four fundamental principles:

1. **Be an owner, not a loaner.** For 200 years, U.S. equities have produced a real (net of inflation) average annual compound rate of return twice that of bonds. In the last 75 years, the equity premium soared to three times. Either the future is going to be secularly different from the past, or bonds are an irrational long-term (much less transgenerational) holding. This is even true – indeed, it's *especially* true – when one is taking income from his portfolio: do you want to try to draw six percent a year from an asset class whose total 75-year return has been about six percent? Or would you think it safer (yes, that's the operative adjective) to try to draw six percent from an asset class whose 75-year return has been 11%?

2. **Make no attempt to "time" the market, nor the relative performance of sectors thereof.** "I have never met a man," Buffett said at his 1987 annual meeting, "who could forecast the market." Assuming (as I do) that this observation was not gender-specific, the greatest equity investor who ever lived is telling us here that we can't time the market. This realization should come not as a challenge but as an immense relief to the career advisor, for it promises a threefold

release of time and energy. (A) She never has to watch the market again, believing that the only consistently "right" time to make a diversified equity commitment is when one has the capital, and the only "right" time to sell is when one needs to withdraw capital. (B) She never really has to watch the macroeconomy, either, since the only pressing reason to do so is to attempt to infer a market viewpoint – which she no longer needs. (C) And most liberating of all, she never has to talk to – much less compete for the business of – crazies who think a portfolio is a financial plan. Indeed, if you just keep talking about transgenerational planning to people with the needle of CNBC in their arms, the crazies de-select themselves.

3. **Don't panic.** In a diversified equity portfolio, price and value are inversely related. Generalized price declines of 30% or so have come along every five years (on average) since the end of WWII; they've always been temporary, and have always been followed by recovery to previously unimagined heights. Buffett "lost" $342 million on October 19, 1987, when his Berkshire Hathaway portfolio declined in price from $3890 to $3180 per share. Last time I looked – less than 15 years later – it was around $70,000. If you don't confuse price with value, and especially if you don't think a temporary decline in the one represents a permanent loss in the other, you won't panic. You won't sell. And you'll be fine.

4. Stay diversified. Forget about higher risk-adjusted rates of return: a diversification discipline is primarily there to keep you from betting the ranch on one spectacular new idea – be it the automobile, aviation, electricity, radio, television, the microprocessor or the Internet. All great technological advances lead – virtually simultaneously – to gigantic leaps in the world's standard of living and to ever more spectacular financial bubbles. Only by lashing yourself to the mast of diversification can you resist the seduction/destruction cycle of each "new era" siren song.

These glorious principles, I say again, govern 95% of a real investor's real lifetime return. The last five percent comes from what I would loosely term "portfolio management" – standard deviation, beta, Sharpe ratio, expense ratio, stars, and whatever other essentially backward-looking analytics are currently in vogue. And where do financial advisors tend to put 95% of their time and energy? Precisely: into the variables which produce *at most* five percent of a client's ultimate return. This *invariably* leads to one or another unthinkable outcome. (How many people pass away each year – intestate, and with little or no life insurance – *while working on their portfolios?*) **Portfolio management almost always misses the point.** But even on those rare occasions when it doesn't, it can never *be* the point.

And so I respectfully ask: would you consider working for the balance of 2002 toward the noble goal of making this *the year you stop managing money?*

Would you, in other words, commit yourself to making your portfolios so goal-focused – so exquisitely attuned to the very longest-term objectives of your clients – that you wouldn't begin to *presume* to tweak them?

My wife and I have a variable universal life insurance policy which will, we hope and expect, fund our estate tax liability when we're both gone – which even a cursory glance at my bride will tell you may not be for 40 years or more. Our 17-month-old granddaughter has a trust fund which may still be growing for *her* grandchildren when she's her grandmother's and my age. What could *possibly* happen in the world and/or the markets over the next year which would warrant a fundamental reordering of these portfolios? Why, nothing, of course. They're soundly diversified; we've been able to add to our holdings at substantially lower prices over the last couple of years; what's the problem?

I'll never understand how looking back at the last year (or two, or five) helps you invest for the next 30 (or 50, or more). I *completely* understand that portfolio turnover correlates negatively with return. I fervently believe that, the closer you can get to that viewpoint in 2002, the better an investor *and* an advisor you'll be. Hippocrates said, "First, do no harm." And I say, "First, *stop managing money.*"

– *NMI*, February 2002

Q&A: THE CLIENT WHO WON'T STOP
DOING THE WRONG THING

Q: *I have been reading your advice about being brutally honest about my book. I have about 25 clients who retired March 1, 2000, at an average age of 55. Most of these clients required distributions from their accounts of eight percent. Now they need more than 10%. I know these people will not make it over the long term unless they stop taking such large withdrawals. Many have said they need the money to live and cannot stop or reduce the withdrawals. They are all in fee-based accounts. I think it's best for me to move on, as they will consume more and more of my time as their financial futures become more dismal. However, I don't feel it's right to abandon them after such a short period of time as their advisor, especially since they have not expressed displeasure about my services. I've considered raising fees, but am concerned they may be willing to pay them and that still won't solve my problem. Any suggestions?*

A: I think you have to start reducing your concerns to writing, both to increase the impact of your advice and, frankly, to create a paper trail – against the possibility that someone elects to blame you when he starts seriously to run out of money. I suggest you write a letter stating your very grave concern that eight percent to 10% withdrawals run a serious risk of exhausting the principal, and warmly encouraging everyone to cut back to no more than six percent of the current account balance. Even that, you must not fail to point out, doesn't guarantee that the account will survive, but it certainly reduces (historically) the risk.

I don't recommend that you fire or otherwise walk away from any of these people, at least for a while, because I think it just increases the odds that one or more of them will turn vicious on you. Having thrown down the gauntlet in writing, you may, I think, just stop calling them and see what happens. If they try to adjust the portfolio in some way, without reducing the withdrawal rate, simply tell them that it is your firm belief that they are merely rearranging the deck chairs on *Titanic*, mark the orders "unsolicited," and update your manager (and the file) as to the content of the conversation.

– *NMI*, February 2002

THE REAL LESSON OF ENRON

We don't have Elian Gonzalez or anthrax anymore, and the 150th nightly "news" report that we didn't catch Osama bin Laden today begins to sound like the old "Saturday Night Live" bit: "Our top story tonight: General Francisco Franco is still dead." So journalism must surely be burning incense to its household gods in thanks for Enron.

This story has everything. Rich people destroyed by hubris, a high-level suicide, document shredding, shadowy ties to the Oval Office – have we so quickly forgotten Marc Rich? – and, best of all, destitute employees whose vaporized 401(k)s were invested solely in Enron stock.

But even as they sift through the rubble, looking for any previously unexamined shard of Enron wreckage with which to fill just one more minute of air time, journalists will never report on the single thing that would surely and certainly have prevented *any* Enron employee from coming to this pass. No, it's not a law, and it's not a regulation. And it isn't even a prohibition against accounting firms consulting for the same companies whose books they audit (*pace* Arthur Levitt).

It's a financial advisor. It's you and me, who were sent into the world to keep people from making The Big Mistake…of which underdiversification is one of the Seven Deadly Incarnations (see *The New Financial Advisor*, p. 234).

No professional advisor worthy of the name would have ever let a client bet the ranch on any one *idea*, much less on any one stock. We may (and we must) conclude, therefore, that all those misbegotten former Enron employees with zeroed-out 401(k)s either didn't have an advisor – which would be a pity – or had an advisor *and chose not to listen to her* – which is a tragedy.

And so you and I must never cease to cry out to America what journalism would rather die than admit: *everyone with money needs an advisor!* Get an advisor! Heed your advisor! Or you will surely end your days in penury, no matter how many legislative/regulatory barn doors the government locks...*after the horse has been stolen!*

– *NMI*, February 2002

CHANGE THE FIRST WORD "SPEECHES" TO "PROSPECT INTERVIEWS," AND SEE IF THIS QUOTE STILL WORKS FOR YOU

"Speeches take place within a context, never in a vacuum. Listeners bring to the occasion not only their own dreams and frustrations, but also a range of questions about the speaker. Who is he down deep? What does he stand for? Does he speak with authority? Does he care about people like me? Can I place my faith and trust in him? Does he have the capacity to make a difference? Who the speaker is speaks as loudly as anything he says."

– David Gergen,
speechwriter and advisor
to four U.S. presidents,
in his book *Eyewitness to
Power: The Essence of Leadership*

Q&A: "GOOD IDEAS" MAKE FOR
BAD RELATIONSHIPS

Q: I just learned that a client I've had for a number of years transferred part of his account to another firm. When I called to discuss this with him, he said he was happy with me and my service, "it just sounds like this other guy has some good ideas." Also, I met with a prospect who has other advisors, but would be open to my ideas. The implication is he would give me part of his portfolio and compare me to the others. How would you approach this?

A: The word "ideas" – as in "this guy has some good ideas," or "I have other advisors but I'll listen to your ideas" – is a code word. Decoded, it means "performance," as in "I have no real relationship with this customer; I live and die on 'performance'."

Your problem is that, consciously or unconsciously, you're still presenting yourself as an investment advisor rather than as a financial planner. Even worse than that (at least in these two cases), you haven't been able to establish yourself as a *goal-oriented* investment advisor. You've let yourself be reduced to the sum of your recent past "performance." This is the worst of all possible worlds.

I don't think your career will acquire any real traction until your product becomes yourself – and, through you, a plan, of which the portfolio is merely a servant. Taking pieces of people's accounts, and being manipulated into participating in a performance derby, is one way to insure that you never achieve this goal.

If I'm following the fact pattern, here, you've already spoken to the "client" once more than you should have. If he transferred part of the account without conferring with you first, you should have taken the account, given it to your manager, and never called – nor taken the call of – this person ever again. Do it now. And forget the "prospect," who is nothing of the kind.

– *NMI*, March 2002

SIXTEEN HUNDRED HOURS

In my book *The New Financial Advisor*, I suggested that, even in your most intense business-building years – when prospecting is (or ought to be) virtually your whole life – you probably can't work more than about two thousand hours a year.

Upwards of a thousand advisors currently subscribe to this newsletter/spot coaching service. And as nearly as I can make you out, you generally seem somewhere between further along and *considerably* further along than the pure prospecting phase. Not that you don't work flat out – you clearly do – but you're making (or seeking to make) more mature judgments about what is equilibrium, what is meaningful work in the context of a meaningful life.

And as you seek an appropriate balance – quality of work and quality of life – I think your gross potential working hours drop off significantly. Once again, it's not that you *can't* work two thousand hours a year, but that you don't care to – not least of all because you feel, quite correctly, that you shouldn't have to. But no matter what their thought processes, my guess is that most serious readers of this resource max out – or should at least be aiming toward maxing out – somewhere around sixteen hundred hours a year.

The questions you have to ask yourself when you come face to face with this number are:

1. what is each one of those hours worth; what, in effect, am I going to charge for it;
2. what do I do to earn (in the sense of deserving) that amount of hourly compensation;
3. what are all the things I must *not* do – because they're not worth nearly my hourly wage;
4. who *should* do what I don't do, and at what wage;
5. what does the number of hours I have to sell in a year – and their price – tell me about how many clients I can possibly serve well?

Let's begin with the last issue first, because it's easy to solve mathematically, and it lets you start backing into some of the other answers. I've always felt that an advisor's span of control – the number of households/families with whom you can maintain anything remotely like a meaningful relationship – was around 250. That almost immediately tells you that you can spare your average client unit no more than about six and a half hours a year. (It also tells you inferentially that you get a huge bang for your buck out of group activities like seminars and Client Appreciation Nights, such that these aren't as expensive as they may at first seem.)

Now let's say that you want to earn $500,000 a year, and that – fully staffed, as you must already intuit you're going to have to be – your practice will need to gross *at least* a million dollars in order to net you half a million. That simply means that the practice is going to have to gross $625 for every one of the sixteen hundred hours you work at it. (It also implies that your 250 families have to be producing an average of $4000 a year in revenues to the practice, so they'd better be both large and complex in their financial needs.)

The questions then become: what do you actually do that's worth $625 an hour to *anybody* – and what endeavors/ tasks must you no longer be involved in? (I once asked an incredibly hard-working, truly well-meaning person what her priorities were. When she passionately answered, "*Everything* is a priority," I knew in that moment she wasn't going to make it. And she didn't.)

Many advisors are quite sure they can improve on their firms' (or their broker/dealers') select list of mutual funds, annuities and such. Even putting aside obvious issues of ego and overconfidence here, is there any compelling reason to think this is a highly value-added use of your time? Are you *that* sure that, 20 years hence, a family will have done so much better than your firm's model portfolios that, discounted back to today, the incremental return will have been *that* much greater than what your time cost them – *and you?*

Or might you better husband their six and a half hours a year for the drop-dead critical task of seeing them, encouraging them, and pouring out your tremendous confidence that your plan – model portfolio and all – is slowly but surely getting them where they need to go?

And if you can buy the freedom and power of a $625 hour

by paying someone else $20 to do in that hour everything you suddenly (and correctly) find unthinkable, what's stopping you? Again, is it economics – or just ego? Thirty-five years ago, I heard big "wirehouse" producers lamenting bitterly that the firm wouldn't get them more help – and I still do. Good heavens: at a $625/$20 swing? Why wait for your firm? Work 90 extra minutes a week – to pay for the entire week of a $20/hour assistant – *but make those 90 minutes count!* (And what's that you say? You can't afford the $20 because you're not grossing $625 yet? If you don't make the investment *now* in offloading all that busy work, you may *never* get there!)

At bottom, all this is only a way of approaching the issue of *running your practice like a business* – indeed, of running it as opposed to letting it run you. Businesses have business plans, budgets and staffing assignments. Nobody in America – and especially nobody in a richly competitive field like ours – runs a successful business by wandering into the office in the morning to see what may happen. And it certainly doesn't work if the boss isn't fully engaged in the highest functions of the business.

You have to have a business plan that you and your staff believe in. And I'm convinced that such a plan begins with the simple act of *fairly pricing your time* – and then devoting that time to making sure that good clients get exceptional value for their purchase of it.

– *NMI*, March 2002

Q&A: THE "ETHICS" OF KEEPING
SMALL ACCOUNTS

Q: *I can't afford to keep hundreds of clients in my book, but firing them seems unethical. When I think about hiring a junior advisor to transfer the clients to, it seems no different from firing them. I work in a small community, so PR is a consideration, or is it? Your thoughts are always appreciated.*

A: The only truly unethical act in this situation is to keep clients you can't serve well. To equate getting a junior advisor, who can give them the time they need, with firing them is a leap of reason which I, for one, can't follow. The right thing to do is to help smaller accounts find the right advisor, either by expanding your practice or by outplacing them in someone else's. And I may be naive, but regardless of the size of one's town, I don't believe doing the right thing ever generates a PR problem of any consequence.

– *NMI*, April 2002

REBECCA'S RIVERKEEPERS

On Saturday, September 16, 2000, I did something I'd sworn never to do again: I deliberately and even joyfully flew in coach class from Chicago back home to New York.

I had hightailed it to O'Hare after my speaking engagement in time to catch an earlier flight. But first class was already booked full – and just this once, that was OK with me. Anything to get me home even an hour ahead of schedule, so that I could rush to the hospital to meet Rebecca Giovanna Dickerson, who'd been born the previous evening.

Rebecca is the firstborn daughter of my firstborn daughter, and thus the beginning of a new generation in the life of our family. Indeed, North America is currently filling up with Rebecca's kind, as the biggest, most affluent group of people who ever lived – the baby boomers – become grandparents.

No matter how long or how eagerly one looks forward to the advent of one's children's children, nothing prepares you – or at least nothing prepared me – for the actual experience. Rebecca has changed the way I look at life – especially at the way the rest of mine might affect hers. And she's clarified the way I think about wealth.

About 70% of all the personal net worth in this country is still owned by the people who made it: it's first-generation affluence. And as one starts putting some net worth together, one tends to think primarily in terms of its supporting one's own later years.

But simply not using up all one's money before one uses up all one's heartbeats begins to seem, after a while, a somewhat effete and perhaps even selfish goal. As our children grow into brave, strong adults with their own dreams and goals – and as our own accumulation disciplines succeed beyond even our expectations – we begin to think of what our wealth might mean to them.

We have to be careful not to let our affluence – and even more, our good intentions – weaken our children. And the best of us are, just as the best of our children are careful to stand on their own two feet and make their own way in the world.

But as our generation becomes first aware and then determined – as we begin to see what a significant legacy might accomplish in the successful lives of our children – we come to regard wealth in a new way.

Rather than looking at money as a finite resource, the chief issue surrounding which is when it will be all used up, we begin thinking of wealth as a river, capable of growing deeper and wider as it flows downstream to the next generation.

And then, in the fullness of time, there is Rebecca – and all the other laughing, wide-eyed miracles of Rebecca's generation. And we start thinking of wealth not merely as transgenerational but *multigenerational*.

We see the river widening and deepening even further, in ways we can't even imagine – because we cannot imagine the glories of the world our grandchildren will live in, any more than my father's father, born by gaslight in the 1870s, could have imagined me and my son flying on the Concorde.

And so we become – her grandmother and I – Rebecca's riverkeepers. We try not to worry too much about whether technology stocks are completely sold out, or about the vagaries of emerging-market investing today, or about how many more lunatics will slaughter their fellow man and claim God's guidance before this is over.

We don't own the river. We see, now, that we're merely its stewards. Although we'll draw water from the river as we grow older, we'll preserve it with an eye toward the days when Rebecca – and her brothers and sisters and cousins yet to be – are our age…and are tending it for *their* grandchildren.

Advisors who like numbers more than they like people always think that money is money, and therefore regard estate planning primarily as a method of saving taxes.

But advisors who bring to their clients the values and skills of the riverkeeper know that money is love. They therefore help their client families see estate planning as a process of widening and deepening – and thereby extending the life of – the river.

Riverkeepers are just naturally going to be better investment clients as well as better planning clients, because they've got the healthiest, longest-term perspective. Make 2002 the year you help your best clients become true riverkeepers.

– *Financial Advisor*, April 2002

EINSTEIN ON WHAT COUNTS

"Not everything that can be counted counts, and not everything that counts can be counted."
— Einstein

Q&A: CLIENTS WHO COME TO YOU
WITH DISEASED PORTFOLIOS

Q: *I have a new prospect who wants someone he and his wife can trust. Among his several advisors, he has more than $1 million invested in 35 different VA subaccounts and mutual funds, and another 12 stocks, a few bonds, and $100,000 in a money market. About 65% of the equities are large-cap value and growth, and 20% or so in mid- and small-cap. There is a lot of duplication, but I hate to make sweeping changes. Would you do major consolidation?*

A: I'd do a lot more than consolidate: I would junk the whole atrocity and make them start over again. This, however, is the smallest issue in the case. Why have they had so many different advisors, and let themselves stumble into this quagmire of a portfolio – and why are they still allegedly casting about for someone to trust? The portfolio is always the mirror of the client, and this portfolio is a godawful, irredeemable mess. Beware this client, and accept the whole account responsibility or no part of it. Good luck.

– *NMI*, May 2002

Q&A: CLIENT LOYALTY IS YOUR BEST (INDEED, ONLY) DEFENSE

Q: *If my colleagues and I all convert to fee-based business, could the firm change our compensation to salary instead of fees?*

A: I don't immediately see why your firm going to salaries would fall more heavily on the fee-based advisor than on the commissioned one. The portability of your book is your ultimate defense, and it's a function of your clients' loyalty to you, which in turn is a function of how well served by you they feel. Since they're obviously better served by the objectivity of fee-based advice, I still think that's your answer.

– *NMI*, May 2002

COACH K ON WHAT TO STRIVE FOR

"My hunger is not for success, it is for excellence.
Because when you attain excellence,
success just naturally follows."

– Mike Krzyzewski, Duke basketball coach,
in his book *Leading From The Heart*

THE ILLUSION OF "RISK TOLERANCE"

One of the most persistent illusions in the practice of financial advice holds that there is, in the dark psyche of each investor, a fixed quantity of something called "risk tolerance."

If it were anything objective – and I don't believe it is – risk tolerance would have to be the percentage decline in the value of one's portfolio which the investor could not (financially, psychologically, or both) bear.

The problem is that none of the assumptions which support the quantity theory of risk tolerance is true. Therefore, pandering to the illusion of risk tolerance – allowing it to become a critical variable in our discussions with our clients – sets everybody up to fail, probably at the worst possible moment.

The flawed assumptions implicit in the concept of risk tolerance include (but are by no means limited to) the following.

1. Risk is synonymous with price decline; i.e. there is only one "risk." This is not true. There are, at the very least, two risks: to principal and to purchasing power. And in the act of mitigating either one of these risks, we increase our exposure to the other.

If I construct a portfolio with the goal of limiting its potential for price declines, I limit to the same extent the opportunity for price advances. That is to say, I compress the potential return. But the more I reduce the potential return, the more I expose it to the erosion of purchasing power, as the nominal return sinks closer and closer to the inflation rate.

The converse is equally true. The more I try to minimize the risk of loss of purchasing power – by making equity investments, whose historical returns far exceed the inflation rate – the more I expose the portfolio to the historical possibility of very large price declines.

The act of trying to find an acceptable middle ground between these countervailing risks is usually (and very unhelpfully) called "balancing risk and reward." This formulation only reinforces the misperception that principal is the only risk.

In fact, what we need to do is balance risk against risk, by choosing which one represents the greater long-term threat to our client family. Then we must move to suppress that more dangerous risk the only way we can: by actively and even joyously *embracing the other risk*.

(A way that you can start to expand your and your clients' Johnny-one-note view of risk is to respond to the question "What about the risk?" with another question: "Which of the two big risks are we talking about, here?")

Above all, there is no such thing as "no risk." This is the great truth that is masked by all the traditional approaches to "risk tolerance."

2. The really important variable in assessing "risk tolerance" is percentage decline. It isn't. It's *time*. Since the end of WWII, the stock market has declined an average of about 30% one year in five. To someone who will need to withdraw significant capital, say, two years hence, this presents a vastly greater risk than it does to someone with no capital needs for 10 years. (Moreover, it may be argued, to the person who never plans to invade principal, but to live on income and bequeath the capital, it represents *no risk at all*.)

Since the risk of holding equities declines very sharply over lengthening holding periods, then, it is *time* which becomes the critical measurement of risk, rather than some arbitrary, pre-set percentage price decline.

Another way of looking at this is to distinguish – again, with time as the operative variable – between risk and volatility. To a 55-year-old couple, whose investments must provide their income for 30 years and more, a 30% price decline (like a 30% uptick) is an incidence of volatility, but not of real risk.

3. An individual's "risk tolerance" is fixed and invariable. It isn't. It rises and falls – quite inappropriately – with the prevailing market trend.

The same people will give you wildly different estimates of their ability to withstand "risk" at different times. This would be bad enough if the public's appetite for risk expanded and contracted contracyclically – i.e. if people got braver the more the market fell, and more cautious the more it soared. But of course they don't.

Consciously or otherwise, most investors' willingness to take on risk rises with the market. That is, as stock prices increase (not just absolutely but relative to value), market risk is clearly rising – but that's just when most people want to be less risk-averse. And when prices are plummeting, instead of rationally expanding their risk tolerance in order to capture rising values, investors run for the hills. It is no coincidence (nor should it be a surprise) that, since the market regained its pre-Crash levels in 1989, the only two three-calendar-month periods of equity mutual fund liquidation perfectly bracket the bear market lows of October 1990 and September 2001.

Thus, at any given moment, an investor's own estimate of his "risk tolerance" will usually be an unconscious (and wrong) call on the current market – and therefore worse than useless.

It remains an uncomfortable fact of life, in these litigious times, that our compliance departments want us to get some kind of handle on just how much tolerance for market ambiguity our clients can muster. But it's incumbent on us to be adult enough to see this effort for what it is: an attempt to put your firm in a position where it can't be successfully sued for failing to gauge just how much adversity a client could take.

But filling out essentially silly forms in order to quantify a will-o'-the-wisp like "risk tolerance" isn't the way to do that. Rather, the answer – as always – is: accept only clients who understand you, and whom you understand. And then just *keep them from getting surprised.*

No surprise, no panic. No panic, no sell. No sell, no lose. *No loss, no lawsuit.*

– *NMI*, June 2002

**PLEASE CLIP THIS QUOTE OUT
AND SEND IT TO YOUR DIRECTOR
OF COMPLIANCE EVERY DAY FOR A YEAR**

"There is no way any professor

or any minister of the church

can tell you what your

risk tolerance must be."

— Paul Samuelson,
Nobel laureate in Economics

Q&A: THE FATAL ILLUSION
OF "ENOUGH INCOME"

Q: *I have a client who is single and 51 years old. Five years ago, she inherited a significant stock portfolio from her father. Currently her portfolio is approximately $4 million and is almost 100% in a diversified managed common stock portfolio. She is thinking of retiring from her job, which pays her $160,000 a year. She mentioned she would like to replace this income by converting into bonds whatever portion of her portfolio it would take to generate the same income. I explained to her that over the long term stocks outperform bonds after inflation by a margin of three to one, and that we could produce the income she needs by slowly liquidating stocks as necessary (for the most part the dividends are offset by management fees). This woman's only heir is her nephew, who is in the same enviable financial position. She has no need for creating multi-generational wealth. In this situation would a balanced portfolio be such a bad idea?*

A: It would, in fact, be an atrocity. You would need to convert more than half the $4 million to bonds in order to yield $160,000. Thirty years from now, when she is 81 and, at trendline inflation, she needs $480,000 of income to buy what $160,000 buys today, how will you advise her? And when the nephew inherits the two million-odd dollars worth of bonds/wallpaper instead of – what? $10 million? $20 million? – that that money might have grown to in equities after four percent systematic withdrawal? He's going to come looking for you with a lawyer if you're lucky and a gun if you're not. Seriously, I can understand a woman with 30 years to live completely missing the point of the erosion of the purchasing power of even a $160,000 income over that time. But it's very hard for me to understand it in an advisor, who gets paid to know better. If this woman insists on committing financial suicide – and, to compound the atrocity, doing it near the bottom of an interest rate cycle – I believe your only ethical choice is to resign the account.

– *NMI*, June 2002

THE COURAGE TO UNDERPERFORM

By the second half of the 1990s, nearly every equity sector and management style other than big-cap growth had stopped working.

Those were the darkening days when the mob was falling ever more deeply in love with the S&P 500 Index – isolating, as the mob has a perfect genius for doing, on the wrong variable. They thought the issue was indexing vs. active management, when virtually all the quite spectacular return of the index was, in fact, coming from about four dozen megacap growth names. Even as "the market" surged higher, it was quite frighteningly narrowing. And then things *really* started to go wrong.

After the brief but devastating Russian default/Asian Contagion 2 bear market of (almost literally) Labor Day 1998, the market resumed its soaring arc – only now, even non-tech growth stalled out. Thereafter, only a dozen or so high-tech big names were carrying the broader market (at the tippy top, tech got to be more than 30% of the S&P 500), and the dot.com mania went into overdrive. You had to have a memory almost longer than mine – back to the heyday of Two-A-Day Charlie Plohn in the 1960s – to remember an even remotely comparable garbage-IPO market.

Simply stated, the last three years of this great bull market – its terminal, bubble phase – were the worst time to be a quality investment advisor that I ever saw, or ever expect to see. If you had an adult memory, a scintilla of historical perspective and/or a care about your clients, you were a wise and valuable citizen. And you were a dead duck.

It wasn't just that the society had bought into the malignant lie of do-it-yourself, and was spitting on advisors – and on advice. Yes, this was the time when information temporarily took the place of wisdom, and nanosecond trading executions on the Internet were more highly prized than patience and discipline. Important as these phenomena were to the bubble, they were symptoms rather than the disease.

The disease, of course, was performance mania, of a virulence that is seen perhaps once every 30 years or so – a generational outbreak. In this extreme strain, the goal is performance at any price – performance which recognizes no other financial or economic risks than being outperformed by the next guy. (Who among us, having heard it even once, will ever be able to forget The Whine of '99: "Everybody's getting rich but me"?)

And, as performance became available only from a fatally narrowing, increasingly homogenous sector of the market, the pure essence of equity investment success – diversification – became first unfashionable, then scorned and punished, and finally virtually extinct. And so it was that, at the historic moment when the *most* capital was *least* widely spread, 80% of it simply disappeared.

Let's be sure, however, that we call the culprit by its rightful name. Yes, tech manufacturers overinvested in their products, projecting dope-smoking demand curves. Yes, in an age where such things were deemed no longer possible, a tech inventory buildup of unimaginable proportions suddenly materialized. And yes, zanier-by-the-day dot.com business models were limitlessly financeable at zero cost of capital.

But it wasn't tech, or telecom, or even dot.com that wiped out a whole generation of performance maniacs. Technology didn't kill people. *Underdiversification killed people.* The maniacs were undone by nothing more than their signal failure to respect the three golden rules of investing in equities: diversify, diversify, diversify.

And what of the quality investment advisor? Those of us with limited enthusiasm for the financial Prozac of asset allocation (and/or whose clients simply can't achieve their goals in anything but equities) must take equity diversification as our virtual religion. But it is a long, dark and lonely road that we walk.

When the market goes down – and especially when it goes way down – no one honors us for limiting the damage to something like that experienced by the general market. If the S&P 500 declines 35% *while the tech sector is down 80%,* we tend to hear from clients only that they've "lost" upwards of 35%...and why didn't we get them out of the market altogether?

But this is nothing compared to the excoriation heaped upon the head of the disciplined advisor when diversification causes clients to underperform – as it invariably does whenever one investment thesis turns into a mania, and thence into a bubble. There are few interactions between client and advisor that are uglier than those which occur when the advisor is trying mightily to save the investor from himself, and the investor is fighting tooth and nail not to be saved.

This conundrum breeds cynicism in weaker advisors. But I'm convinced that it only makes the best of us even more committed to doing the right thing. And with diversification, as with virtually every other important aspect of investing, the right thing comes down to two bedrock behavioral principals: managing expectations and preventing surprise.

You can't – and would never want to – change the *financial* experience of being a diversified equity investor. That experience means being too spread out to catch the full effect of one soaring sector/idea. Thus it means consciously and deliberately underperforming some highly publicized, red-hot investment thesis – perhaps for years. And what good is that?

Of course: the bright side of diversification is protection from overexposure to one sector/idea when it crashes – or just drifts through years of regression to some trendline return. Diversification, then, when it's done right (as opposed to: I'm diversified because I own 78 different tech stocks), is *the conscious choice not to make a killing in return for the all-important blessing of never getting killed.*

But that financial experience isn't ultimately what counts. (What really happens is never what counts.) The only things that matter are (a) is what happens consistent with the expectations the investor was given, and therefore (b) does the investor or does he not get *surprised* by what happens? For, in the end, the least surprised investor will always get the best returns.

It is, I admit, perfectly true that a broadly diversified equity portfolio will ultimately get the investor the full return of all the component equities, without – at any given time – the full volatility, because different portfolio components will be running on somewhat different cycles. And therefore, I even more grudgingly concede, real diversification delivers, over the very long haul, a higher risk-adjusted rate of return…whatever that means. (I'm 35 years in this business, and I can remember doing some things years ago that I'm not 100% proud of. But at least I've never said "higher risk-adjusted rate of return" to a poor, defenseless American family. And believe me, that's something to cling to as one grows older.)

But the decision to forego making a killing in order not to

get killed is an emotional and even moral choice rather than a calculating, intellectual one. And when you're going through a protracted period of "underperformance," that decision sometimes has to be reaffirmed every day. That reaffirmation – against all one's screaming urge to just go chase the hot dot on the scattergram – is a truly heroic act. *They don't call it "the courage of one's convictions" for nothing.*

At the end of the day, diversification is there to lash the investor to the mast, so that he can't answer the siren call of the "new era" *du jour*, and be wrecked upon that fatal shore. But you, as the advisor, can only tie him up with his full knowledge – and indeed at his request. And then, you can't let him bully you into untying him.

And some days, that takes all the courage you've got.

– *Financial Advisor*, June 2002

Q&A: ACKNOWLEDGING YOUR MISTAKES

Q: *I attended your recent Master Class® and found it very valuable. I am implementing many of your ideas. One in particular is investing 100% in equities. I'm having trouble conveying this principle to clients, since I've spent the last 10 years recommending asset allocation. I now believe clients must own 100% equities if they are to build wealth. If I share this new belief, will my clients be confused or lose confidence in me? What approach should I use to get my clients 100% in equities and decrease the chances of my clients losing faith in me?*

A: The short answer to the narrow question is no: I don't know of any particular way of "spinning" a great – indeed, *the* great – investment truth in such a way as to "decrease the chances of (your) clients losing faith in (you)."

The larger issue, of course, is: why *would* the communication of a great – indeed, *the* great – investment truth confuse or upset your clients in such a way as to jeopardize the relationship? (Unless, of course, the "relationship" is already fatally compromised.)

That question is, in any event, ultimately academic, since you don't have the option of withholding the truth from your clients once you've discovered it. You can't let people continue to labor under a delusion in order to "save" the account. That's immoral. And tomorrow, another advisor with more courage will tell your client the truth, and you'll lose the account anyway.

You are not the first advisor to build a career on asset allocation only to discover that it's a bad bargain; you won't be the last. Personally, I would have no trouble saying to a client, "I hope you know that I never stop studying my craft, which is positioning my clients to have the greatest probability – historically, at least – of achieving their financial goals.

"Up until recently, I've believed that asset allocation – spreading my clients' assets among stocks, bonds and cash, primarily to mitigate the volatility of the equity market – was the best course. I no longer believe this.

"I now believe that asset allocation, in shielding you to some extent from the equity market's temporary volatility, also cuts you off from the permanent incremental return of equities. This has come to seem to me more and more to be a less than rational strategy.

"Historically, investors who've been willing to ride out the equity market's occasional sinking spells have been rewarded with significantly higher returns. Indeed, over the last three-quarters of a century, the equity investor has earned a real return – net of inflation – nearly three times that of the bondholder.

"I believe we should consider permanently increasing our portfolio exposure to equities – not as a 'call' on the market, but out of a healthy respect for the historical realities – and as a meaningful boost to your chances of achieving your longest-term financial goals. This is a serious step, and I'd like the opportunity to talk it through with you (*optional*: and your family) face-to-face."

Prior to this meeting, I'd send the client my book *Simple Wealth, Inevitable Wealth*, asking that he particularly read Chapters Two, Three and Four (An Owner Not A Loaner; What The Real Risk Isn't; What The Real Risk Is). I urge you to read the corresponding chapters – for the advisor's eyes only – in *The New Financial Advisor* (Chapter Six: The Brain Of Financial Planning; Chapter Seven: Doctor Noah's Rx For **Real** Safety And Income; Chapter Eight: Doctor Noah's Fee, And What It Pays For).

An advisor who doesn't grow and change is a bum. A client who won't let his advisor grow and change is a "relationship" you *want* to end. Read Emerson's essay "Self-Reliance." Tell the God's-honest truth all the time, and let the chips fall where they may.

– *NMI*, June 2002

NAUGHTY, NAUGHTY

Donald, you are a good boy. But you have done a naughty thing. You must stay after school, and write on the blackboard 100 times: "There is no statistical evidence for the persistence of performance."

"According to Morningstar, one-star funds have outperformed five-star funds by 45% since 1995. If you invested $1000 across the universe of one-star funds in January 1995 and then moved the proceeds each year to the then-current crop of one-star funds, your investment would have been worth $2948.54 at the end of 2001. If you'd pursued the equivalent five-star strategy, you'd have $2030.48."

– Fortune, July 8, 2002

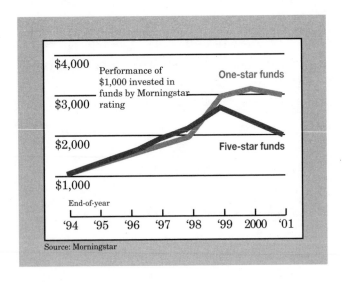

Source: Morningstar

TWO CAUTIONARY RULES
FOR OPENING NEW ACCOUNTS

The late stages of a great bear market are always a golden time to be expanding one's practice. Amateur advisors are finding their true calling in the management training program at Starbuck's, and quitting the field in droves. The chastened do-it-yourself investor is at last seeking advice. And, amid widespread capitulation, professional advisors are busily helping equities to return to their rightful owners at 1998 prices.

At a time like this, the maximum number of sadly disappointed accounts is up for grabs. This is both the good news and the bad news.

The good news should be obvious, and is beyond the scope of this brief discussion. The bad news – or perhaps just the cautionary news – is that you're going to run into a fair number of accounts that are available, all right, but for the wrong reasons and/or on the wrong terms. I just want to raise two red flags, here, as to accounts you mustn't accept.

1. Take over the management of the whole portfolio or no part of it. An advisor returning to the profession after a hiatus recently did a close reading (a bit too close, I think) of my 1996 book *The Excellent Investment Advisor* side-by-side with its successor *The New Financial Advisor*, published last Thanksgiving. He was struck by the fact that in *EIA* I made a huge issue of not taking pieces of accounts – of not allowing clients to have other advisors to whom you'll constantly be compared, usually unfairly – but that in *TNFA* I made little or no mention of this particular issue.

I was philosophical about this. If one refines one's philosophy in book form every few years, one is alternately suspected of re-hashing, and then dinged if one didn't. But I digress.

Don't take pieces of accounts. Don't subject yourself to "competing" advisors. In *EIA*, my code word for this was **Eisenhower**, based on a story that the politics of WWII were such that the idea of splitting Ike's command surfaced at one point. Eisenhower said he'd continue to bear the whole responsibility or none of it, and the bad guys backed down.

Go thou and do likewise. It never works. It always ends badly. Portfolio management is a means to the end of the client's financial planning, not a performance derby. Stand up for the integrity of the stewardship: one plan, one planner.

2. Only cash gets on the Ark. Do not let people bring you their bombed-out '90s portfolios, their huge chunks of appreciated stocks that they "can't" sell, or some other advisor's pet mutual fund/stock portfolio.

Accepting this kind of account is mission impossible: you're taking responsibility (if only moral responsibility) for a lot of stuff you may know little or nothing about, but your authority to mold the portfolio is severely constrained. *Responsibility without authority is a fool's errand*; get both or neither. Waive any commission and sell it all out.

Nor do I want to hear any guff about taxes. No investment should ever be held because of the investor's tax consequences. How many people do you suppose have seen 40%-90% of their portfolio evaporate over the last 30 months because they wouldn't pay 20% long-term capital gains taxes? One shudders to think.

Will it be "harder" to get new accounts if you accept these two disciplines? I guess so, but then excellence is always "harder" – until you achieve it, if only in your own mind at first, whereupon it becomes effortless. And since, to readers of this resource, mediocrity is unthinkable, your only real choices are excellence and quitting.

Don't let anyone get you without getting your portfolio. And don't "compete." It's beneath your dignity.

– *NMI*, July 2002

WE INTERRUPT OUR ROUND-THE-CLOCK COVERAGE OF THE APOCALYPSE *DU JOUR* TO BRING YOU THIS STARTLING AND WONDROUS TRUTH

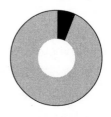 **Global population
6.0 billion**
U.S.: 4.7%

 **Global GDP
$31.4 trillion**
U.S.: 31.2%

 **Global spending on
R&D (48 countries)
$652.7 billion**
U.S.: 40.6%

All statistics for 2000. Sources: UN, World Bank, IISS, Institute for Management Development.

– *NMI*, August 2002

TECH: A VIRTUOUS CYCLE

Two events – both guaranteed to warm the heart of a grateful recovering technophobe like me – took place virtually simultaneously during the week after the July 4th holiday. Gordon Moore was awarded the Presidential Medal of Freedom. And Warren Buffett made his first investment in the technology sector.

You will remember that the most transcendent anecdotal irony of the tech bubble was that Nasdaq made its all-time high – and Berkshire Hathaway its panic, value-is-dead low – on the very same day. Buffett had eschewed tech, and been roundly ridiculed for doing so, on the absurdly unfashionable grounds that he would not invest in businesses he did not understand. (A similar stick-in-the-mud prejudice on the part of the public at large might have saved it – just to pick a number off a bus – three trillion dollars. But I digress.)

On July 8, Buffett's Berkshire Hathaway put $100 million into a $500 million pool, with Legg Mason and Longleaf Partners, to make a nine percent convertible loan to the fiber optic cable company Level 3 Communications. This debt is convertible at $3.41 a share, which is close to what the stock was trading at before the deal was announced; it immediately went up about 50%. (On paper, this gave the Buffett syndicate an 18,250% annualized return. But I digress.)

At this sublime moment, when portfolio managers are afraid they'll get fired if they're caught buying tech stocks, and you couldn't raise a dollar of venture capital for a tech startup anywhere in the lower 48, along comes Buffett. And just as we look back at Berkshire Hathaway's capitulation low as a perverse indicator of tech's top, I have little doubt that its first foray into tech/telecom will sooner than later be seen as a sign of tech's impending bottom.

Gordon Moore, blessings and peace be upon him, is the co-founder of Intel who postulated in 1965 that the power of a computer chip would double about every two years. And so it has done, to a fare-thee-well, ever since.

But Moore's Law, as it's come to be known, is much more than a staggeringly prescient technological observation. It describes a virtuous cycle, one that is very pertinent to an understanding of where we are at this moment.

Looking back at the American experience over the last year and a half, we see, in effect, two separate, disconnected economies. One is the consumer economy, and if there has latterly been a recession in this country, the consumer has yet to hear of it. Unemployment seems to have peaked at around six percent – there are those of us who remember when that was a floor, not a ceiling – and consumer spending has held up wonderfully well, largely thanks to developments in the housing market. With the price of his home rising sharply, and with interest rates cratering to the point where he could extract a lot of that increased equity without increasing his monthly mortgage payment, the consumer has been a happy camper indeed.

The *business* economy has, on the other hand, been a disaster, with plunging corporate profits causing massive cutbacks in capital investment in general and technology spending in particular. But IT-driven productivity is surging, and that's causing a recovery in profits, which will ultimately lead to new technology investment.

Meanwhile, Moore's Law marches on. The relative price of computers to a unit of GDP has fallen by half just since the beginning of 1999. Bear Stearns' John Ryding recently wrote of this trend, "As the price (and size) of computers to a unit of GDP falls, new opportunities to embed technology into products that were previously seen as nontechnology goods grow and, thus, new markets for technology goods are created, *which in turn can enhance the growth rate of productivity*" (emphasis mine). And there you have the pure essence of a virtuous cycle.

I'm not suggesting that it's time to take a second mortgage and buy the Q's here. But I do believe that, just as technology's power was wildly overestimated 30 months ago, its great and fundamental transformative effects on our economy are currently being not just underestimated, but ignored.

– *NMI*, August 2002

Q&A: MORE ON DISEASED PORTFOLIOS

Q: *As part of client reviews and when opening new client accounts, I make sure that clients are diversified and, if not, reallocating. However, I have taken some heat from colleagues who are incredulous that I would do this when a fund or funds might be down. To me, it is never the wrong time to do the right thing. I see their point as being no different than trying to time the purchase of an investment. What say you?*

A: I say pretty much exactly what you say. "Down" from what? The investment doesn't know you own it; it isn't going to behave any differently whether you're "up" or "down." If it's the wrong thing for the client to own, or to own quite so much of, there is no wrong time to sell it, and to re-deploy the capital into something he should own – which, although this may not have occurred to your astrophysicist colleagues, is also "down." What do these advanced thinkers recommend? Holding the wrong investment 'til the client gets even...by which time the right investment will have gone up just as much, if not more?

– *NMI*, September 2002

Q&A: ON REBALANCING

Q: *What is your opinion of rebalancing?*

A: It makes my eyes glaze over. It's one of the last, desperate repositories of the vain hope that you can meaningfully affect a client's return by portfolio management...by *doing something*.

For people who are adding regularly to their investments during the accumulation phase of their lives, dollar-cost averaging is rebalancing for you. In static portfolios, even reinvested dividends and gains are rebalancing, by the same DCA logic. Finally, in the longest-term sense, regression to the mean is rebalancing.

All of that said, if regular (say, annual) rebalancing of a static portfolio makes you and/or the client breathe easier, be my guest. The key word in the foregoing sentence is, of course, **regular**. If you're rebalancing at odd intervals, whenever it *feels* to you like things are out of whack, you're actually market-timing and trying to kid yourself about it, and you're going to go straight to hell.

– *NMI*, September 2002

THE MARKET DOESN'T KNOW
WHERE YOU BOUGHT IT

Much of my e-mail traffic manages sooner or later to introduce as an important datum how far today's prices are below what clients paid. Advisors talk to me about the percentage decline in their clients' holdings, or how much their investments have to go up to "break even," or the fact that, having used up their money market war chest, systematic withdrawers are now having to sell fund shares "at a loss."

I can't think of any more irrelevant investment statistic, nor one less helpful in making an informed decision now, than your cost. Cost has absolutely no bearing on an investment's current value or future behavior. Simply put, the market doesn't know where you bought it, and wouldn't alter its behavior one iota if it did. How, then, would your cost become a useful input into today's decision-making? Of course: it would not. Consciousness of your cost can never help you, and there are lots of ways it can really hurt you – or rather, enable you to hurt yourself. Markets, after all, don't kill people; people kill themselves, often by obsessing about totally meaningless "measures" such as their own personal paper "loss."

If you bought a Renoir in 1950 for a million dollars, and it's now worth $80 million, that's a certain kind of experience – but it doesn't change the nature of the painting, and it doesn't affect the current price. If you bought the same Renoir in 1989 for $100 million (because you had to bid against half a dozen Japanese) and it's now worth $80 million, that's a different kind of experience – but the painting is still the same ineffable work of art, and its current (and future) price is totally impervious to your cost.

Welcome to the doctrine of sunk cost, which simply states that once you buy something, your original investment is gone, and the value of your asset is entirely a function of (a) its capacity to produce an income and/or (b) what someone else will pay you for it today and tomorrow.

Andrew Carnegie was touring his brand-spanking-newest steel mill one day with his normally ebullient second-in-command, Charles M. Schwab. Schwab was diligently showing off the plant, but his boss sensed a certain lack of enthusiasm, and asked why.

Schwab sadly told his chief that he wished they'd started to build this mill 18 months later, because some improvements in manufacturing that had come along in the interim would have meaningfully lowered the price at which they could profitably sell their steel.

How much lower would these recent innovations drive their cost, asked Carnegie, and Schwab replied, "At least five dollars a ton." Carnegie immediately ordered Schwab to tear the mill down and build the more modern one. He knew that the incremental volume which would flow to the low-cost producer would pay for both plants many times over. And he knew that if he didn't harness the latest cost-saving technology, his competitors would, and thereby render the mill in which he was standing worthless, irrespective of its cost.

Now, neither the Renoir painting nor the Carnegie steel mill is a perfect analogy to your clients' depreciated equity portfolios. But they do at least suggest the danger implicit in allowing sunk costs to cloud people's minds, much less dictate their decisions.

Look: the broad stock market declined by nearly half, peak-to-trough, in the last 30 months. *Everybody's* under water; the only question is by how much, and the answer is usually: quite a lot. It isn't as if your clients have been somehow singled out. A bear market of this length and/or depth is an equal-opportunity crucible.

Forget your cost. Look relentlessly forward, never backward; assume you bought everything you own as of last night's close. Were that the case, the prospect of another 10% or 20% down wouldn't disturb you very much. You'd probably say: I like these prices, these valuations and even these yields. I think the huge preponderance of the bad news (and, even more so, of the market's capacity to be shocked by any remaining bad news) is behind us. I think too many people are bearish, that huge net liquidations of equity mutual funds are a contrary indicator, and that, somewhere along in here, the economic and earnings surprises will start to be positive ones. Freed from an unhealthy obsession with my cost, I can see clearly that selling a stock market that yields nearly two percent to buy "safe" five-year government debt that yields little more than three percent almost has to be a terrible trade. With equity, I at least have a chance to rebuild my capital; with three and four percent debt, I have none. *I'm not happy with the way I got here, but I'm stoical about where I am.*

Advisors, I believe, have a right and even an obligation to begin shutting down clients' perseverations about their sunk costs, and to suggest that they regard their current capital base as a starting-over point, replete with tomorrow's possibilities rather than with yesterday's regrets. Thinking about what a diversified equity portfolio might be worth five and 10 years hence, instead of what it was worth three years ago, is more than the beginning of successful investing. It's the beginning of emotional maturity about the equity market, and thus the beginning of wisdom.

— *NMI*, September 2002

TUNA FISH REDUX

Back in 1994, when a fairly mild six-month market down-turn was being greeted as the incipient end of the world, I did a magazine column in the form of a short, light-hearted seminar. Called "The Great Value Rally of 1994" – to make the point that all generalized price declines are ultimately rallies in value – this seminar preached a parable: that the kingdom of investment heaven is like unto a can of tuna fish.

Late in the summer of 2002, with the broad market down nearly 50% from its peak, I thought it was time to update this piece, to contemplate that millennial bear market.

As the text makes clear, you have to be very careful not to let this presentation exacerbate the audience's natural pro-clivity to try to time the market. But when done the right way, this seminar communicates the great truth that price and value are inversely related – a concept that is mostly lost on most Americans mostly all the time.

SLIDE ONE

The Great Value Rally of the New Millennium

Folks, thanks very much for coming to our seminar to-night. We're excited about the terrific opportunities that the current environ-ment presents – not least of all because most people *aren't* excited. Most folks are scared...which tells you that it's way too late to get scared.

You see, if most folks were right, most folks would be rich. Since most folks sure aren't rich, we at (FIRM) like to try to figure out what most folks are thinking. Then, we enthusiastically recommend that our clients and friends go out and do the opposite.

Our theory is that most folks are very aggressive when it'd really pay to be cautious, and very cautious when it's time to be bargain hunting. Clearly, it's bargain hunting time. We call it The Great Value Rally of the New Millennium.

You see, in the world of investments, when the *prices* of investments go down, the relative *values* of those investments go up. Most folks don't see that. They love it when prices go up – even though that usually means value is going down.

SLIDE TWO

When Prices Go Down, Values Go Up.

For instance, suppose you know of a stock that's going to earn $5 a share this year. We'd advise you to love that stock at $40, tolerate it at $80, and look for something else to buy at $100. Because as the *price* goes up, the *value* of that same $5 in earnings is being ground down.

Most folks, of course, are hiding in the basement at $40...and taking a second mortgage to buy with both hands at $100. They seem to forget that, in investing as well as every other aspect of their economic life...

SLIDE THREE

High Prices: Bad. Low Prices: Good.

(Advisor reads the slide, then invites the audience to read it aloud with him.) Yes, high prices: bad. Low prices: good.

That's the guiding principle of all economic behavior... *except in investing.* (Note: if the audience hasn't started chuckling by now, you're in trouble. If it hasn't started laughing out loud by the end of the next slide, you're dead.)

You see, most folks would never behave in a supermarket the way they do with their investments.

SLIDE FOUR

TUNA

What are you paying for a small can of tuna fish in the supermarket these days? (Audience agrees on a number; say $1.39.) OK, now suppose you walked in tomorrow and saw a big sign:

SLIDE FIVE

TODAY ONLY
Manager's Special
TUNA FISH:
$4.89 a Can!

(Advisor reads Slide Five.) Well, you'd probably squint at it for a moment, figuring the fella might have just misplaced the decimal point, or something. When you realized the sign was right, you'd have said thanks, but no thanks: (1) that's way more than the usual price range, and (2) there's a half dozen other protein sources in the supermarket that you can substitute for tuna, at a calorie-equivalent price of $1.39, right? In effect, you'd have said, "high prices: bad."

Naturally, everybody had the same reaction, and now the market is stacked to the rafters with unsold cans of tuna. Now the manager has to mark 'em down and move 'em out. So the $4.89 is crossed out, and now it's 79 cents. What do you do? Back up the truck, of course, before the guy changes his mind, and before your neighbors buy all the tuna. What's happened? He's lowered the price...and rallied the value! LOW PRICES: *GOOD!*

SLIDE SIX

TODAY ONLY
Manager's Special
TUNA FISH:
79¢ a Can!

Can you see where we're going with this? Sure you can! Everybody was wild to buy stocks when the S&P 500 was at 340 in August '87. It was a NEW HIGH! Uh-oh; most folks forgot. High prices: bad!

Well, quicker than you could say "tuna fish," it was October 19, one of the biggest one-day value rallies of modern times. Indeed, it was probably the sale of the century – 20% off the great companies in America between sunup and sundown – something you see once in an investing lifetime. Overall, the market went down about a third in just three months. *And most people hated it!* Seems they forgot: LOW PRICES: GOOD!

SLIDE SEVEN

S&P 340 · August '87
High Price: Bad!

S&P 230 · Oct. '87
Low Price: Good!

Wouldn't you know it? The S&P went up about 60% from those lows, and it did so in just less than three years. And folks loved it! Just couldn't get enough. Iraq massing troops on the border of Kuwait? Hey, no problem. Those folks are always squabbling with each other about something.

SLIDE EIGHT

S&P 370 · June '90
High Price: Bad!

S&P 230 · Oct. '87
Low Price: Good!

Well, sure enough, we had an invasion in the Middle East, an oil price shock and the onset of a fairly serious recession all at once. And, once again, tuna...uh, sorry: *equities*...went on sale – 20% or so in just one turning of the leaves of summer into fall. And most folks got paralyzed.

You're getting the hang of this – I can just feel it!

SLIDE NINE

S&P 370 · June '90
High Price: Bad!

S&P 295 · Oct. '90
Low Price: Good!

Well, I don't have to tell you what happened next, do I? From October 1990, with just one 15% setback in the summer of 1998 that I'll bet hardly anyone remembers, the price of tuna fish – sorry, there I go again: the S&P 500 – *more than quadrupled* in less than 10 years…to its all-time high of 1525 in March 2000. (The price of red herring – uh, Nasdaq – actually went up 10 times in the same period.)

> **SLIDE TEN**
>
> **S&P 1525 · Mar. 2000**
> **High Price: YECHHH!**
>
> **S&P 295 · Oct. '90**
> **Low Price:** ~~Good!~~
> GREAT

And so it was time for a *millennial* tuna fish sale.

Historically speaking, this was a heck of a sale: almost half off from peak to trough.

> **SLIDE ELEVEN**
>
> **S&P 1525 · Mar. 2000**
> **High Price: YECHHH!**
>
> **S&P 780 · Oct. 2002**
> **Low Price: WOW**

The last one of those we had was in 1973-74, and the one before that was the greatest sale of all time – 1929-32 – which bottomed out around 5 on the S&P 500.

OPTIONAL: Now maybe, before this is over, they're going to mark the tuna down a bit more. (1) We don't know. (2) Nobody else does either. (3) That's not the point!

The idea here isn't to try to time the market, or to look to get out at market tops and back in at bottoms – something which nobody, and I mean *nobody*, can consistently do. What we're trying to do is get you to see that most folks behave toward the great companies in America in a deeply counterintuitive way. When prices are marked way up, people love it and can't wait to buy more. When prices are marked down, people are scared to death. Not only don't they want to buy any more tuna fish, but they're seriously thinking of selling what they already have in the pantry.

And so, the moral of this story is: *it's all tuna fish.*

All investments are cyclical. When prices are high, and everybody loves 'em, that's the time to be disciplined, stay diversified, and stick to your long-term accumulation plan. When prices are low, and headlines are scary, most folks don't want 'em. And that's where, historically, the great opportunities lie.

SLIDE TWELVE

Moral:

IT'S ALL

TUNA FISH

What are we selling tonight at this seminar? Nothing in particular – except plain common sense, and the courage to zig just a little, when "most folks" around you are zagging. We'll be happy to take questions now.

This seminar has proven to be phenomenally effective over the years, if only because it helps people remember to laugh at their fears during tense times in the markets. And I promise they'll remember you for giving them permission to lighten up a little.

– *Financial Advisor*, October 2002

RAISING EXPECTATIONS

Were the stock market to reach its March 2000 peak in five, seven or 10 years – and assuming dividends, growing at their trendline rate, are paid out – total equity returns from the S&P 500 would run in the range of 9.3% to 16.1% a year. The Ibbotson trendline return, even assuming the *compounding* of dividends, is 10.7%. So if this superbear market's recovery time is about the same as that of comparable episodes, we're in for a protracted run of average to above-average returns.

I don't hear a lot of people saying that. Hell, I don't hear *anybody* saying it.

Remember, this isn't a prediction. It's merely a recitation of highly comforting historical fact: savage, once-in-a-generation bear markets have usually been followed by periods of very nifty returns. Either this time is different or...draw your own conclusions.

If your conclusions are anything like mine, now would be a good time to start really talking them up. Because there's so much doom and gloom around – and it's so pervasive – that you could get to be a pretty big hero over this next little while, simply by helping people not completely miss the boat. Because, left to their own devices, completely miss the boat they surely will, if recent ICI mutual fund sales/redemption figures mean anything. Which they do.

In July, $52.63 billion was net-redeemed out of equity mutual funds. This is the largest one-month stock fund outflow in history. Added to June's $18.28 billion net redemptions, the total of nearly $71 billion is, not surprisingly, the largest two-month withdrawal ever.

But hey: I can vividly remember, in 1968, when all the equity mutual funds in the U.S. of A. didn't have $50 billion *in* 'em. So the whole number can't mean that much. To see how bad these two months really were (or weren't), you have to look at the percentage of all stock fund assets that these huge redemptions represent.

No help; the news is just about as bad as it gets. July's $52.63 billion flight was 1.7% of total stock fund assets, which isn't quite the worst month ever. But you're not going to be happy when I tell you what month holds the record. It was, of course, October 1987 – arguably the worst month to sell in the history of the Republic – at 3.17% of total stock fund assets. (June and July 2002, at 2.1% net redemptions, stand second only to October and November 1987, at 3.7%.)

Now the news really gets bad. You see, bond funds – not money market funds, bond funds – had a record $28.14 billion net inflow in July. The previous record was $16.71 billion in August of last year. And now, hold onto your hats: year-to-date through July 2002, bond fund inflows of $86.57 billion are only a hair less than *the record full-year inflows of $87.7 billion in (you guessed it) 2001.*

The mob thinks that bonds are going to provide a better return, over this next block of time, than will stocks. The mob is not usually right. Now is the time to set your face sternly against the mob, and to earn treasure on earth and in heaven thereby.

At the Battle of New Orleans, when the Americans' first artillery volley went completely over the advancing British lines, Andrew Jackson is supposed to have said, "Reckon you better elevate them guns a little lower."

It's been years since I've said this – and for a while I wondered if I'd ever get to say it again – but I reckon you better elevate people's equity return expectations a little higher. And maybe a lot higher.

– *NMI*, October 2002

THE BLAME GAME: 2002 EDITION

"The Spitzer investigation is a curious exercise. It doesn't clarify history so much as distort it. It portrays the financial losses of countless madly greedy, very knowledgeable speculators as a kind of theft by a handful of people who acted in bad faith....

"The whole of the muckraking machinery is designed to facilitate this simple inversion: the culprits of the 1990's, reckless speculators, are being recast as the victims. What the various investigations appear to be doing is cleaning up the markets and making it safe for sober investors. What they are actually doing is warping the immediate past and preserving investors' dignity along with their capacity to behave madly with their money the next time the opportunity presents itself."

> – Michael Lewis
> "The Vilification of the Money Class"
> *The New York Times Magazine*,
> Sunday, October 27, 2002

THE SEDUCTIVE FOLLY OF MARKET TIMING

You had to know in your bones, as the first buds showed on the branches early in 2000, that we were in the last stages of the greatest investment/financial bubble of all time.

I certainly did. Indeed, I wrote a piece for a Canadian magazine in January or February in which I said, among other things, that all (repeat all) of the capital raised in dot.com IPOs since the beginning of 1999 was ultimately going to be lost. My only problems were (a) I couldn't figure out what if any effect the bursting of the tech bubble would have on the overall market, and (b), much more to the point of this essay, *I had no idea when, nor from what level, a decline would begin.*

So I had to be content to sit there, with my very well-diversified portfolio (which was, *ipso facto*, very underweighted in tech), determined to ride it out. Not, heaven knows, because I wanted to, but because I know from bitter personal experience that I can't time the market. Such stalwarts as Warren Buffett and Peter Lynch say they can't either – and all three of us are on record as believing that no one else can, at least not consistently.

My own pathology with respect to market tops has historically manifested itself as being right, but way too early. Now, you're only as sick as your secrets, so let me come completely clean on this issue, and confess that there is another name – more accurate if less charitable – for "being right, but way too early." It's called Being Wrong. Hi, I'm Nick, and I'm a grateful recovering market timer.

In the interest of my therapy – and, I hope, yours – I would like to describe how I hit bottom: the point at which I became sick and tired of being sick and tired, and resolved never to try to time the market again, one day at a time.

In the fall of 1986, when our tenures at Bear Stearns overlapped, the economist Lawrence Kudlow began raising red flags, even as the market continued to surge. Gold prices, commodity prices and interest rates were all beginning to rise meaningfully; Kudlow said that if they kept doing so, eventually they'd break the bull market's back.

They kept doing so. Kudlow's warnings became ever more strident – while the rabble were shouting that it was OK that our market was selling for 22x earnings, because Japan's was selling at 45x! Finally, in the spring of 1987, I couldn't take it anymore, and sold just about everything I had except my newly public Bear Stearns stock. The market immediately rocketed to wildly higher highs for the next three or four months. Finally, in August, it topped out.

Of the inglorious denouement to this story, little need be said, mostly because you've already anticipated it. I'd sold in the expectation of a crash; what I got was no less than the greatest one-day crash in U.S. stock market history –

and I was lucky to buy back my portfolio about where I'd sold it, and poorer by the round-trip commissions. (I did manage to put in a whole bunch more money – much of it borrowed for the occasion – post-October 19, but never mind that.) I've never been tempted to market-time again.

And thank heaven I haven't, because if you ever read my 1995-98 magazine columns in *The Craft of Advice*, it's clear that I thought the market might be smoking a controlled substance from about Dow 4500 on up. And that was before dot.com.

I was reminded of this the other day as I watched a CNBC interview with the great Robert Shiller of Yale, who in April 2000 published the classic book *Irrational Exuberance*, which dispassionately and devastatingly documented everything that was wrong with the market.

And what about your own portfolio, the interviewer asked. Shiller said he started selling in 1997, and was completely out by the end of 1998.

Can you believe it? Here's the guy whose book made one of the greatest market calls of all time – *and at the pluperfect moment*. And if he's lucky, he's now getting to buy his portfolio back **just about where he sold it!**

Let that be a lesson to you, boys and girls. At this juncture, when advisors and clients alike are saying of the recent unpleasantness, "There *had* to be a way to know;

there *had* to be an exit strategy; buy and hold just *can't* be the only answer," you must stand firm against the siren call of market timing.

Churchill once said that democracy is the worst form of government ever devised by man – except for all the others. That's pretty much how I feel about buy and hold in properly diversified, professionally managed portfolios. Buy and hold is absolutely the worst equity investment strategy ever devised by man – except for all the others.

– *NMI,* October 2002

WILL YOU BE AN OPPORTUNIST OR A VICTIM?

Like a hurricane, this once-in-a-generation bear market will have spent the huge preponderance of its force quite a bit before it actually blows itself out.

Waiting for the market to bottom – or, far worse, for the consensus to agree that it's bottomed – is the final act of victimhood for an advisor. And it assures that he'll remain far behind the curve when the recovery takes off, reacting instead of acting, which is itself a guarantee of mediocrity.

But the superior advisor, no matter how badly her existing business has been hurt, will intuitively see the potentialities inherent in the devastation of the last few years. And she'll resolve to rise above her current difficulties in order to capitalize on a career-making confluence of opportunities which – like the bear market that spawned it – comes once to each generation of advisors. The night-and-day difference in what is about to happen to these two advisors is neither financial nor economic but purely attitudinal. And, as always, it will be the opportunists who sup upon the bones of the victims.

Of the market itself, little need be said. This time isn't different (except perhaps in one very positive, very hopeful sense, which I'll touch on in a moment). This is the fifth generalized market decline of roughly half (or more) in the last hundred years. The last one was in 1973-74, when the S&P 500 declined in 22 months almost exactly as much as it's declined in the last 30 months. Very long, very powerful bull markets that climax in great, speculative, "new-era" blowoffs usually die in great violence and pain. This is no exception. In time, the markets (and the economy) clean out the excesses, and resume their perpetual advance from much lower, healthier levels; those prices are never seen again.

(The great, positive difference I perceive in this cataclysm is that it seems much more a financial than an economic event. As I was at some pains to document in my newsletter this month, the four other superbears of the last 100 years – 1906-07, 1919-21, 1929-32 and 1973-74 – took place against the background of the most extreme economic and even social devastation. The worst this downturn could manage was a 0.7% recession in GDP in the first three quarters of 2001 – which was more than made up for in the fourth. While we decry the slowness of the recovery, note that it is recovery's velocity – not its existence – which most reasonable observers debate. The current bear market thus strikes me as much more a correction of bubble excesses, returning the market to its 1997-98 levels, than a discounting of fundamental economic reversal.)

In any event, the market will finish going down when it's finished going down, probably sooner than later. When you have a month like July 2002, which saw both the largest one-month net liquidation of stock funds in history *and* the largest one-month net inflow into bond funds, you can assume that the hour of your deliverance is somewhere at hand. As in the first quarter of 2000 – which featured a month when aggressive growth fund inflows exceeded those of *all other equity fund types combined* – the mob very rarely acts with such unanimity, and is always wrong, usually very quickly.

But that's not the issue. The behavior of the market can neither be predicted nor controlled, so it mustn't be allowed to run your career, much less your life. Your own behavior, on the other hand, is virtually the only thing you can control – and therefore your beliefs and actions over this next block of time will make or break you.

Herewith, some attitudinal/behavioral adjustments which, should you choose to adopt them, have the power to propel you to the top of the advisory profession as the economy and the markets resume their historic and permanent uptrend.

1. Start closing the door on your regrets. The best of us tend to take our clients' financial and emotional distress very personally – particularly when we feel complicit. It was we, after all, who urged them to commit their long-term future to equities. And perhaps we feel we should have fought them harder when they wanted to get overconcentrated in tech and telecom.

Well and good. But complicity is one thing; cause is another. We didn't *cause* this market disaster, in which even the best-diversified equity account has declined nearly 50% from the March 2000 peak. The destruction is universal.

Get over it. Start by dealing proactively with people who keep tearing you up about their "losses" in pretty much the same words every time you talk to them. Offer to have one final sit-down to go over these issues, see what can be learned from them, and move on. Get closure, or get gone. Guilt and recrimination are not bases on which productive relationships can go forward. And you need to go forward, with your current clients or without 'em.

2. Embrace the great lessons you've learned from this bear; rejoice that you never have to learn them again. In investing, as in life, it seems we have to learn all the really important lessons the hard way. Somebody must have taught my training class that you never bet people's whole portfolios on one idea, but I still had to go out and buy the Nifty Fifty growth stocks in 1971-72 – and see 'em go down 80%-90%, while the broad market only declined by half, in '73-'74. They were my generation's dot.com.

Somebody must have told us that all commodities cycle, and that all cartels fail – but I had to go out, believing that with OPEC "this time it was different," and bet the ranch on energy-based inflation in 1978-80...just before oil, in inflation-adjusted terms, spent the next 15 years going back to its 1973 price levels.

I get it now: you never lose faith in mainstream equities; you never get underdiversified, you never bet the ranch, and this time is never different. Go thou and do likewise. Great lessons, learned the hard way, make great advisors.

Some other lessons you should have learned from this conflagration:

(a) Don't just be an investment advisor; you'll end up riding this roller coaster for the rest of your life. Be a financial planner.

(b) Don't let clients beat you up into letting them do the wrong thing, under the explicit or implicit threat of taking their business elsewhere. It's the ones who bullied you into letting them go whole hog into tech, telecom and especially dot.com who got hurt the worst – and may now be giving you the most *acita*. Next time – and all the other next times – stand by your guns, and if they're going to walk, let 'em walk *before* the spaghetti hits the fan. It'll save you untold grief. And it'll make you proud of yourself.

(c) Try to help people not to learn too much from any one experience. Mark Twain said that a cat, having once walked upon a hot stove, would never walk upon a hot stove again – *nor upon a cold stove*. In that sense, I wonder if the stock market isn't turning into our Great National Cold Stove. (Those bond fund net inflows certainly suggest that it might be.) Keeping your equity portfolio diversified, no matter what, is learning not to walk on a hot stove again. Asset-allocating a large portion of your portfolio out of equities to protect against volatility – at or near the bottom of an interest rate cycle – may be more of a cold-stove lesson. Especially if, in fleeing equity volatility, investors cut themselves off from the returns they're going to need in order to fund a dignified, independent retirement.

(3) Encourage clients to forget about what their investments cost. The third step in liberating yourself and your clients from the pain of the last few years is to help them forget about what they paid for their portfolio. Cost is almost never a useful datum in making good investment decisions.

It wasn't that long ago that advisors were constantly running up against investors who "couldn't sell" wonderfully appreciated but underdiversified holdings because of the capital gains tax. (Never mind that being able to keep 80% of the fruits of successful risk-taking is about as close to real fairness as the U.S. tax code ever gets.)

Well, having to bear onerous taxation on their gains is an issue that's now completely gone away for most folks. So how come they're not happy? Right: now they won't face reality and intelligently rebalance their portfolios because they "can't take the loss."

At the tail end of a once-in-a-generation bear market, your cost becomes just another way of making yourself nuts. Your investments don't actually know what you paid for them, and wouldn't behave any differently if they did. Why then do we burden our portfolios with psychological implications which they refuse to bear? (Daniel Kahneman just won the Nobel Prize in Economics for answering that conundrum, among many others.)

The only sane test of a portfolio's merit is: do I believe that, going forward, my investments are likely to achieve my and my family's long-term financial goals? Only an affirmative answer to that question is a rational basis for holding (much less adding to) a portfolio; "I can't take the loss" is merely a denial of reality.

Sit down with your clients and review their portfolios by, in effect, marking them to market as of last night's close. That is, assume your clients bought everything they own off yesterday's net asset value.

You don't have to like where you are – and no equity investor does, which should actually be some comfort: your client certainly hasn't been singled out. But you do have to accept the reality of where you are, and assess your holdings from a goal-focused perspective rather than through a painful haze of essentially self-induced regret.

Have one last conversation with each cost-obsessed client. Accept responsibility for your part in his decisions –

but from this point on, reject blame. (They're very much not the same thing.) Review what you've learned together; see what if any useful course of action can be inferred from what you've learned. And then move forward with that client – or move on without him.

The three essentially backward-looking lessons of this essay so far are aimed at helping your existing client base make peace with what's happened to them – and at helping you make peace with those clients, and with yourself.

But, as difficult as it may be for you to accept, your existing book (or what's left of it) probably isn't the key to what's going to become of your career. It's all the *other* advisors' clients, as well as a whole generation of chastened do-it-yourselfers, who are more likely to be critical to the trajectory of your success as we come out of the current nightmare.

I've made some of the following points in other contexts in these columns, but please bear with me as I attempt to reorganize (or perhaps just repackage) them into a for-ward-looking attitude/action plan whose goal is to engi-neer a quantum leap in your client/asset base.

(1) The victim will go on reacting to how upset his clients are; this will paralyze him. The opportunist will act on how upset everybody else's clients are;

this will vault her to a whole new level of productive activity. The message of this essay so far boils down to two essential values: (a) perspective and (b) closure. This time isn't different. All great lessons have to be learned the hard way, but then never again. Let's learn what we can, accept where we are, and move forward.

Today's once-in-a-career opportunity, for the quality advisor, begins with a sense of wondrous joy: look at all the financially and psychologically damaged people out there who've been abandoned by their callow advisors, *or who threw themselves upon the sword of do-it-yourself.* What an enormous amount of good you can do just by being the clear, empathetic, optimistic and caring voice of reason.

From 1997 through 2002, the American stock market basically round-tripped. My guess is that half the people who became advisors starting in 1997 – and a third of those who were already advisors in 1997 – will be gone when this is over. (Indeed, from the fall of '87 until the end of '90 – the last time we had a crash, a recession, and a "war" with Iraq – that's exactly what happened.)

That natural orphaning process, augmented greatly by the death of the illusion of do-it-yourself, is creating life-changing opportunity for somebody. If your clients are really upset *and you're still talking to 'em,* imagine how betrayed and abandoned clients feel by advisors who've ceased to function, or simply disappeared. These clients are the millennial lost sheep; will you be the shepherd?

(2) At this exact moment, the biggest, richest generation that ever lived is in a pre-retirement panic – especially because financially they lost the last five years. The first huge wave of postwar baby boomers is just now reaching age 55 – and they don't know what hit 'em. Fifty-five is the beginning of the end of any meaningful pre-retirement planning that's ever going to amount to anything. And when you've round-tripped the previous five years, you're about as susceptible to sound advice as you're ever going to be. History has delivered the baby boom generation to the opportunistic advisor on a silver platter; it doesn't get any better than this. No, wait; actually, it does…

(3) The great timekeeper in the sky just blew the two-minute warning on the baby boomers' parents. Show me an American 55-year-old, and I'll show you a 78-year-old couple who started him the night the old man got home from the service after the Second World War. Which means that Dad and Mom were born in 1924. Which means they came to consciousness in – and were psychologically/financially formed by – the Great Depression.

Which, in turn, means two very important things. (A) They don't just have more money than they ever thought they'd have when they were 23; they have more money than they knew was *in the world* when they were 23. (Start with a $750,000 house they own free and clear, that they bought for $13,000 in 1948 on the GI Bill, and that Dad's been improving with his own hands ever since.) (B) They don't know how to talk to their kids about money. Money was something *their* parents whispered about in fear, late at night when they thought the children – today's 78-year-olds – were asleep.

This is where – and, even more importantly, when – you come in. You see, the great mass of the baby boomers' parents will be going to their reward between 2008 and 2013. And their kids don't know what the plan is – partially because Mom and Dad can't talk to them about money/ death...and partially because *there is no plan*. This next half a decade is *their* last chance to plan. But it's only going to happen if a caring, sympathetic advisor goes in there and gets everybody talking – if only to her. The next time you turn around, this opportunity will be gone, because these people will be gone. And finally:

(4) This is the perfect moment to be joyously pounding the table. When this market finally turns, you'll never see these prices again, and a year from now – two at the most – you're gonna look like a big, big hero. At this point, you have my permission to tell people to stop worrying about the market going down the last 20%-30% with them in it. Instead, be afraid – be very afraid – of the market going up 100%-200% *with you out of it*.

The last time the market declined this much was 1973-74. It bottomed at 588 on the DJIA – and then proceeded to go up 20 times in the next quarter century. Some day, some way, this is going to happen again. Be the opportunist whom a grateful generation of wealthy Americans remembers as "the person who simply refused to let us miss it."

Because I promise you, boys and girls: demographically, economically, financially and career-wise...when this train pulls out of the station, it ain't ever coming back in your lifetime. **So be on it.**

– *Financial Advisor*, November and December, 2002

Q&A: YOU CAN'T HELP CLIENTS
WHO DON'T TRUST YOU

Q: *A 59-year-old client, planning to retire in two years, recently hit the panic button and bailed into a money market account. I recounted this story to my wife and told her that after talking to this client six different times over the past year and a half, I was letting the crazies jump ship. She chastised me for not having more compassion and holding people's hands, telling me that it's my job and that I should put myself in their place. Needless to say, we had a debate. Should I have more patience? My wife claims no one completely trusts anyone, including their doctor or CPA. My position is that I can't work with people who don't trust me. Am I wrong?*

A: I am delighted to report that you are 100% right and that your bride is 100% wrong. (She is also logically inconsistent: if "no one completely trusts anyone," how would any amount of incremental compassion and/or hand-holding close that gap?) Six conversations in 18 months is way above and beyond the call of duty; thereafter, if someone goes screaming over the gunwales of The Ark, you are not only without blame, *you are without responsibility.* Say it loud, and say it proud: "I can't work with people who don't trust me."

– *NMI*, November 2002

THE NINETIES:
DECADE OF GREED OR DECADE OF GREATNESS?

Something made me go back, one day last month, to one of my all-time favorite books: Robert L. Bartley's *The Seven Fat Years*. Written during and after the bear market and recession of 1990-1991, the insider trading scandals and the collapse of the savings-and-loan system, *The Seven Fat Years* had a simple and compelling premise.

Bartley said that the Boeskys, Milkens and Charles Keatings – and everything they stood for – were being used as effigies. Their malefactions helped press and public to characterize the 1980s as a sham: a decade of greed and corruption, in which a grotesquely inflated stock market bubble sucked in and destroyed the little guy while enriching a few junk-bond criminals.

The Seven Fat Years said: not so fast. The 1980s began with a resurgent Federal Reserve throttling inflation to death, proceeded through a revolutionary program of tax cutting to vanquish the stagnation of the '70s and reignite economic growth in this country, and ended with final victory in the Cold War. Real GDP grew by a third from 4Q82 to 3Q90, and the U.S. created more than 18 million jobs during those years.

Bartley's book is a complete history of what we may fairly call the Reagan Revolution, and a blueprint for its renewal.

But the hook was: don't just look at the decade's (temporarily) ugly denouement; look at the miracles wrought during the decade as a whole.

Now, anyone who writes – or engages in the creative process in any form – will tell you that one's unconscious is grinding away at whatever you're working on, even when you're not aware of it. And I know what sent me back to Bob Bartley's book when I (consciously) have so much else to read.

Simply stated: **it's happening again**.

The Enrons, Arthur Andersens, WorldComs, Dennis Kozlowskis, Jack Grubmans and Martha Stewarts, together with the implosion of dot.com and the tech/telecom depression, have been more than enough to convince Americans that the bear market of 2000-2002 is the final judgment on *another* "decade of greed." Forget that the broad stock market tripled from 1990 to 1998, in this view. Concentrate on the fact of the horrific round trip since then. Because it confirms that the whole decade was pretty much a fraud.

In fact, it does nothing of the kind. It was the stock market that got way ahead of itself, with a "new era" pipe dream that drove the cost of capital in the tech sector to zero, and set off exactly the same frenzy of overinvestment that's torched every breakaway technology in the last 200 years – from canal building to railroads to automobiles to airplanes to radio to television to microprocessors to the Internet.

But if the stock market became an illusion that tripped out on its own hype, the real economy of the 1990s was (and remains) a cornucopia of astonishing achievements.

It wasn't all that long ago, for example, that everyone from serious mainstream economists to television talking heads debated where the NAIRU was. The Non-Accelerating Inflation Rate of Unemployment was held to be the point of equilibrium full employment. If unemployment kept falling below the NAIRU, we were assured that inflation would inevitably flare again. There was no question that NAIRU was real; the only issue was where the demon lived.

But as Chuck Yeager intuited about the sound barrier half a century earlier, NAIRU turned out to be a figment. The 1990s were the decade in which we achieved unemployment below four percent while the core inflation rate hovered between two percent and three percent.

This synthesis was the great economic breakthrough of the decade. And although we've backed off it some in the tech-driven recession, the fact that it *can* be done almost certainly means that it will be done again – that we can view it as a norm and not an impossible dream.

(And the datum that we've shed 1.4 million jobs since year-end 2000, as reader Pat Gorkow recently reminded me, shouldn't be allowed to obscure the fact we're still up about 16 million jobs from 10 years ago – nearly 35 million in the last 20. We were and are a beacon to the world in this regard.)

And when unemployment falls as far as it did in the '90s, the benefits of economic growth broaden out in the population, especially among less-skilled workers, who are suddenly in a lot of demand.

Wage increases for the average worker surged ahead of low inflation after 1993. The Census Bureau says that real median household incomes were up seven percent from 1990 through 2001. But the gains were much bigger for minorities: 20% for blacks and 15% for Hispanics.

The poverty rate fell from 13.5% of the population in 1990 to 11.7% in 2001, says the Census Bureau. But again, the big gains came where they were needed most: the black poverty rate, which had been over 30% since the Bureau started keeping the numbers, began dropping precipitously around 1995. And, in spite of a small uptick in 2001, it ended that year at 22.7%. Predictably, first-time home ownership soared.

The re-acceleration of productivity was another big economic story in the later '90s – and it has continued apace, even in the teeth of recession. Just in the last three quarters (since the recession ended), productivity has blazed, growing at a 5.8% annual rate for nonfarm business and 6.9% for nonfinancial corporations.

And productivity is simply the key to everything. It grows earnings even where there is no pricing power; it sharpens America's competitiveness in world markets; it attracts new investment; and it allows workers' wages (and living standards) to rise without impinging on profitability. Even I don't think anything like five percent and six percent productivity gains are sustainable. But it's clear that longer-term productivity is progressing on a sharper curve than the tepid rates of the '70s and '80s. And I do agree with Greenspan's sense that perhaps only half the IT-driven productivity improvements embedded in currently available technologies had gotten into the supply chain before the draconian cuts in investment in 2000-2001.

Finally, there is the miracle of the Internet itself. Nascent in 1990, and not even printing on Bill Gates's radar screen (by his own admission) as late as 1995, the Internet now connects the world – intellectually, financially and culturally. If nothing its believers thought about investing in the Internet turned out to be true, *everything (and much more) that they thought about the technology turned out to be right as rain.* And as anyone who's tried to get (and stay) on AOL lately knows, that technology is still in its rubbing-two-sticks-together-to-make-fire stage. Imagine even a Zippo lighter....

I've argued at length in this resource that the bear market of 2000-2002 is very much a financial event rather than an economic event. I would have you take this essay as, in effect, the completion of that thought. The stock market bubble (with the frauds, cooked books and appalling overinvestment that drove and were driven by it) has been righteously consumed by fire and the sword.

But the unprecedented – and even undreamed of – economic advances of the 1990s are still standing, and indeed ready to resume surging forward. *Pace* Bill Gross, the real risk is not that the market will go to 5000 with you in it.

The risk is that it'll go to 15,000 with you, and your clients, out of it. And then keep going.

– *NMI*, November 2002

REAL ESTATE IN THE REAR-VIEW MIRROR

The November 2002 issue of *Financial Advisor* magazine carried an ominous squib under the headline "Investors Look To Real Estate To Outperform."

It seems that an outfit called Behringer Harvard Funds, a commercial real estate investment company, commissioned a survey by Opinion Research Corporation of 400 investors who had made at least one stock, bond or mutual fund purchase/sale outside a retirement plan within the last two years. The survey was conducted in September – when, as you'll recall, the stock market was once again in free fall.

The 400 respondents (75% of whom, the survey found, use a broker or financial advisor for some or all of their investment advice) were asked to predict which asset class would outperform the other over the next three years: real estate or "the stock market."

A terrifying 45% predicted that real estate would outperform over the next three years, while an even more blood-curdling 12% – one respondent in eight, gentle reader – said the stock market would do better. (God knows what, if anything, the remaining 43% said. The brief summary in *FA* doesn't say, which may, upon mature reflection, be a mercy.)

This confirms an anecdotal impression I got when I was

on the road speaking to advisors in September and October. When not worrying about, and I quote, "the housing bubble," my audiences wanted to know how I would handle an objection they'd been hearing a lot: "I'm putting all my money in real estate."

Now, before plunging on, let me recite my bias(es). Real estate is my second favorite asset class in the whole world – after equities. First of all, operating real estate *is* equity. It's a business which lends itself to increasing cash flows – and therefore capital values – over time, as rents rise. Second, it offers very meaningful equity diversification, in that while stocks (and bonds too, of course) correlate negatively with inflation, real estate correlates positively with it.

Finally, real estate offers you ways to make money when inflation/interest rates are rising or falling. Inflation/interest rates rise, new construction slows/stops until rents rise enough to justify the higher development and debt service costs; thus owners of existing property enjoy increasing rents/cash flows over their fixed-rate mortgage expenses.

Inflation/interest rates fall, rents don't go anywhere, but capitalization rates – the yields real estate trades on – may decline, and therefore prices rise (not unlike bonds). Even if cap rates stick, and cash flows tread water, lower interest rates may give real estate owners an opportunity to refinance and pull out a lot of equity without a taxable event. What's not to love?

(One caveat: the foregoing relationships have historically prevailed in that wonderfully, fearfully illiquid asset called operating real estate. And I assume they prevail in the *long-term* prices of REITs, which – like the prices of any publicly traded equity – must ultimately converge with the value of the underlying assets/businesses. I'm a lot less sure that REIT prices are anywhere near this rational in the short run – but then, what stocks are? Short- to intermediate-term, I suspect REITs trade more like bonds, with the current dividend as, in effect, the coupon. If and to the extent that's true, and you think we're near the bottom of an interest rate cycle, it would make you a little queasy about the next move in the prices of REITs. But I'm getting ahead of myself.)

A telling oddity of the Behringer/ORC study is that, when it asked people to rank the importance of real estate investment objectives, capital appreciation came in first, cited by 40% of respondents. Income (11%) finished a poor fourth, behind portfolio diversification (31%) and capital preservation (15%).

This reminds us that Americans don't really understand operating real estate, in which the capital appreciation potential *is* the income, in effect. Since investment real estate trades on its income – rather than on its replacement value, as people's homes do – the 40%/11% disconnect cited above confirms that investors tend to get their overall view of real estate investment from what's been going on in the price of their home(s) lately. That may be a mistake.

And looking at home prices vs. the stock market in the rear-view mirror, in order to form a view of the three-year relative future of these two asset classes, is almost certainly a mistake.

Unless his worst instincts are reined in by a competent and caring advisor, the American investor is a veritable demon extrapolator. Show him the trend of the last three years and he will assure you that that will be the trend of the next three. By the end of 1999, when only growth investing in general – and tech/telecom/dot.com in particular – is "working," while value lies bleeding into the carpet, the pathologically trend-following investor will bet the ranch on tech growth.

And in late 2002, when real estate has been shooting the lights out for three years while the stock market has been getting killed, a survey like this will find four times as many people predicting that this trend will remain in force as it does people betting it'll go the other way.

This is certainly not me talking down real estate. This is simply me saying: the red hot asset class of the last block of time is highly unlikely to be the big winner of the next. If history (rather than permanently bent investor psychology) is your guide, you'll incline to the belief that the beaten-up, devalued asset class of the past few years has the real upside potential, just as the everybody-loves-it, much more fully valued, darling asset class of the last several years is probably fixing – relatively speaking, at least – to struggle.

And when a reasonably scientific sample of Americans prefers one asset class to another by 45% to 12%, you can assume that that's heaven telling you to go the other way.

Granted, if people are going to invest in *anything* instead of equities, I'd a jillion times rather have it be real estate than bonds. But I'd most prefer they not avoid equities in the first place. And so should you.

– *NMI*, December 2002

GOOD IS THE ENEMY OF GREAT

"To go from good to great
requires transcending
the curse of competence."

— Jim Collins, in his book
Good to Great

BEHAVIORISM TRIUMPHANT

I was extremely fortunate, in the mid-1980s, to attend a presentation by Daniel Kahneman and Amos Tversky, who in 1979 had published a landmark paper in *Econometrica* on decision-making under uncertainty. Their work became the foundation for the whole field of behavioral economics, which studies (among other things) the fundamental non-rationality of investor decision-making.

At that stage of my career, modern portfolio theory was in the first great phase of its ascendancy. I thought (and think) modern portfolio theory absurd; its acolytes remind me of nothing so much as people who clung to Newton's physics even after Einstein.

Like Newtonian physics, modern portfolio theory was and is extremely attractive, because it seems to explain everything, and moreover to explain it in a wonderfully simple and readily comprehensible way. The only trouble with both systems is that each is premised entirely on one idea which is manifestly untrue.

Newton's physics assumed that the universe is finite and in a stable state; Einstein demonstrated that it is neither. Modern portfolio theory begins with the idea of the rational actor: that all market participants are rational, self-interested and calculating. All my experience suggested just the opposite – that the great mass of individual investors were non-rational (and even systematically nonrational) in their behavior. But I couldn't find my Einstein...until I encountered Kahneman and Tversky, who knocked me clean off my horse on the road to Damascus.

My career since then, both as an advisor and now as an advisor to other advisors, has been based on the realization that investment performance (a) can't be predicted, (b) can't be controlled, other than through the asset allocation decision stocks/bonds, and (c) doesn't matter. The vast preponderance of an investor's lifetime return comes not from investment performance but from investor behavior, and that, I found, was something over which I could exercise some meaningful control *if I worked on it pretty much full-time.* This meant that I did virtually no "portfolio management" – which was just fine, because I'd decided it was mostly a waste of energy anyway.

I've never, from that day to this, suggested that the funds/managers I chose were going to outperform those owned by my clients' neighbors. Instead, I've maintained that *my clients were going to outperform their neighbors.* The trick has been getting them to see that these are two entirely different things.

The reason we were going to get better results than virtually the entire rest of the investor population, I said, was that we were going to behave more appropriately than that same percentage of investors. Not so much by doing something exceptionally, brilliantly right, but by avoiding the Big (Behavioral) Mistake.

In a very real sense, Kahneman and Tversky gave me permission to concentrate my career as an advisor on the effort to modify investor behavior. And, to the extent that you've been a consumer of my written and/or spoken work since about 1990, I've mostly been passing that permission on to you. So I invite you to join with me in celebrating the fact that, on October 9, Daniel Kahneman was awarded the Nobel Prize in economic sciences. For, in validating behavioral economics, in some very small way the prize validates your efforts and mine. (One can only mourn, as Dr. Kahneman always does, Amos Tversky's terribly untimely passing in 1996. He was by all accounts a mensch's mensch, and would surely have shared the prize had he lived.)

Forget markets; forget relative performance. Get your own psychology under control, and then concentrate on helping clients to behave appropriately – or just not to behave inappropriately. And you'll have more than riches: you'll have happiness.

– *NMI*, December 2002

A NEW YEAR'S RESOLUTION:
NO MORE CASTING PEARLS BEFORE SWINE

You're sitting with a prospect. Or, worse, you've already gotten a new account. You've analyzed his situation carefully, listened empathetically to his biases/fears/misconceptions about money and investing, and developed a clearly thought-out strategy for him to pursue, under your guiding hand. You lay it on him. He say no, and gives you a lot of half-baked reasons as to why not (or maybe just: why not now). Or he flat says you're wrong. Or he simply says he'd never do what you're recommending ("Most/all of my long-term capital in equities? Fahgeddaboudit!").

What do you do now?

My e-mail traffic from subscribers to this resource (as well as a lot of stuff that comes washing in over the transom) divides up into three general categories: (1) prospecting anxiety; (2) insufficient knowledge of (and/or loss of faith in) basic economics and the workings of the capital markets; and (3) the frustrations and self-doubts which advisors experience when they're trying to help people who resist help.

My response to the last issue has evolved a lot over my career. Thirty-five years ago, when I was training to be a commission-based, market-focused, "performance"-driven

New York stockbroker, I was taught that whatever the prospect said negatively was an "objection" and that my job was to "overcome" it. This process was called "selling" – which, in practice (in New York, at least), was a not particularly subtle euphemism for "arguing." (Ah, but I was so much older then; I'm younger than that now.)

"Selling" (in the old sense) was a fairly stupid way to run a business, but then consider the essential stupidity of the business itself: trying to convince people that you knew when the market would go up, and which stocks would go up the most or the soonest, and other things that (although I didn't know it at the time) could simply never be true.

But as I progressed from selling stocks/products to managing portfolios and ultimately to true financial planning, the need to "sell" – to convince people who resisted doing the right thing – began to wither away. Except on those occasions when it didn't.

That's when I found my competent, caring, empathetic self casting my pearls before swine. And then I had a decision to make, just as you do when faced with the fact pattern in the first paragraph of this essay. Luckily, this decision is basically binary: you only have two choices. Alas, as with so many issues in this business (and in life), the easier of the two choices is most often the wrong one.

The easy/wrong choice is to start "selling": trying, in a very good cause, to overcome the "objection(s)." Of course, you can change the experience of this ignominy by calling it by a prettier name: "reasoning" or, heaven help us all, "educating." Words like this cast a warm glow over the process, and help us not to notice that the prospect isn't reasoning back (now *he's* arguing), and/or that he very clearly doesn't *want* to be educated, because *he already seems to think he knows more than you do.*

Why do we kid ourselves about people like this? Why do we expend our precious time and energy trying to help people who clearly do not want to be helped, or at least not by us? Above all, why do we generate toxic levels of self-recrimination when we "fail" (and that's the word we use) to convince people to follow the right course of action?

The answer, of course, is that the other alternative seems (unconsciously) to be more painful. It's walking away from the dysfunctional prospect you have, and putting the effort into the anxiety-producing but ultimately far more rewarding work of seeking the prospect you really want.

All human beings seek to minimize pain and stress. Faced with two painful/stressful alternatives (continuing to try to reason with Jabba the Hutt, here, or walking away and prospecting for a really good client) we will, with no conscious thought, choose the one we *perceive* as being less painful *right now.* So here we sit, showing Jabba (accompanied by the ravishing Madame Jabba) the Ibbotson chart. They might be swine, but they're the swine we've got, at the moment. And that certainty, distasteful as it is, wins out over the even more daunting uncertainty of prospecting. So we go on casting our pearls before dysfunctional people.

Make 2003 the year you stop doing this. Wrangling with psychologically unsound prospects is an unconscious confession that we lack faith in ourselves – faith that, if we keep showing our superior wares to enough people, we'll ultimately attract the right kind of passenger to our Ark.

And that lack of faith is a downward spiral: give in to it today, and you'll feel even less faith in yourself tomorrow. You can't afford that. Even more important – unless you disagree – *you don't deserve it.*

You can accept what you have, or you can go after what you deserve. It's a choice, and sometimes you have to make that choice every day.

But if you can consciously look across at a querulous, indecisive or argumentative prospect and say, "I deserve better than this; let me use my capacities in a healthier way," then you can really start to close the gap between where you are and where you want to be at the end of this year.

We all *say* we believe in ourselves. Make this the year you truly act on that belief. Make this the year you begin to get the practice you deserve – by acting as if you deserve it.

– *NMI*, January 2003

NO TIME FOR "HEROES"

As part of the spot coaching service I offer subscribers to my newsletter, I very often get questions that start off looking like portfolio issues, but end up being inquiries into a peculiarity of the advisor's psyche.

Recently, I received an e-mail from a very conscientious advisor with a client who had 55% of his invested net worth in 16 stocks. While acknowledging that he had too many beans in too few buckets, the advisor then launched into an inquiry into *managing the capital gains tax liability*. She even went so far as to wonder if the recent election results might lead – some day, some way – to an overall reduction in capital gains taxation.

At first glance, this appears to be a simple situation in which there are two variables, and the advisor has misguidedly elected to focus on the wrong one.

Here's a client who's terrifyingly underdiversified, in stocks neither he nor the advisor actively follows, or even knows that much about. And here's a client who'll have to pay (given his basis) about 16% of the current value of the portfolio to get completely out of the stocks and be free to diversify properly. *And the advisor is agonizing over the taxes.*

But I think there is a deeper and more common issue here, which has nothing to do with the facts of the case. Simply stated, this advisor is trying to be a hero, instead of just playing the percentages that must make her client successful over time.

The essential impulse to try to be a hero springs from two sources, one of which is very noble and the other very dumb. But the melding of these two disparate drives functions pursuant to a kind of psychic Gresham's Law: the dumbness drives out the nobility, so that the net result is purely dumb – and ultimately counterproductive.

The noble impulse is, of course, to want to do superior work for our clients. The advisor we've just discussed seeks to time the realization of capital gains – apparently not realizing that that way lies timing the market – and even tries to anticipate the future course of tax legislation. Other recent subscriber inquiries have focused on valuation as a guide to where the market might turn, or the enhanced returns that might be available from alternative investments, or what sectors/styles might lead the next major market advance. All stem in part from the laudable desire to do a great job for the client.

The dark side of this force is rooted in the commission-driven, "performance"-dominated business model, in which the advisor seeks to produce superior returns as a way of keeping his current clients and competing for new ones. This is the dumb impulse: the advisor as drug dealer, saying, in effect, "I'm gonna get you higher."

The fusion of the noble and the dumb always ends up in the same place, in that all of the methods of potentially skewing a portfolio's return above the trendline also run a commensurate risk of skewing it below.

Now, those of us who build our clients' portfolios in whole or large part on the backs of active managers live with this iron law every day. And presumably we've made our (and our clients') peace with that decision.

But just beyond that basic, binary (active/passive) issue lies another question. To wit: *is this the time* to be sticking our clients' necks out, straining for "extra" return at the risk of missing some significant part of what history tells us will be a powerful post-bear market recovery, characterized *in and of itself* by above-average returns?

That's a very long, very important question, and just before I send you back to read it through once more, let me arm you with my answer: not on your nellie.

Normal recoveries from bear markets of the kind we've just been through tend – especially in the early years – to be periods of very handsome returns. Moreover, these kinds of returns usually come as a very pleasant surprise to many or most investors, whose expectations have been exaggeratedly depressed by the bear market just past. Moral: assume you can earn people above-average returns, *and delight most of them in the process*, simply by hitting the ball long and straight down the middle of the fairway.

You not only don't need to do anything fancy, in this view: you shouldn't try.

And in practice, you're going to have more than enough difficulty just getting people back into properly diversified, long-term goal-focused (as opposed to backward-looking market-focused) portfolios, in the months – maybe even years – ahead. As I suggested in this space last year ("The Courage to Underperform," see page 133 of this book), the establishment and maintenance of adequate diversification is, in a very real sense, the ultimate act of heroism.

Nor does almost anyone need above-average (i.e. "heroic") returns in order to achieve his long-term financial goals. If all you ever get from equities is the Ibbotson trendline seven percent above inflation – and/or three times the real returns of bonds – what else do you really need? And in a country whose economy is the whole world's growth engine (and whose dollar is the whole world's reserve currency), can anyone seriously doubt that the next 50 years are going to be at least as productive as the last?

Do you want to be a hero? Financial planning is heroism. Not altering your plan or your portfolio every time the wind changes direction is heroism. Faith in the future is heroism. *Saving people from themselves is heroism.* But trying to squeeze out a couple of extra percentage points of return by being really "right" about something – at the risk of being really wrong? Well, I'm not sure what that is. But it's not heroism, at least not the way I understand it.

This is the time of year when advisors are hard at work on their business plans. And to the extent that you want to make a plan for 2003 that has the best chance of success, you won't bet the plan on one prospect, one product, one manager or even one practice management strategy. You'll play the percentages. And, even more to the point, you'll advise clients to do the same.

Resolve to make this the year you stick to strategies that historically get the most people most of the available returns most of the time. Will some people drift away from you, and will there be some prospects you don't capture, because your approach isn't exciting enough? Surely the answer is yes – and these are exactly the kinds of people you didn't want anyway.

Make a comprehensive, written plan for people. Fund the investment portions of that plan (mutual funds, annuities, variable life) with diversified, professionally managed equity portfolios. Don't try to time the market. Don't panic. And, once diversified, stay that way: don't bet the ranch on a "new era," be it technological or financial. Don't chase "performance."

If you will simply do everything in the foregoing paragraph, and never compromise those principles, your clients will end up no lower than the 95th percentile of all Americans in terms of total lifetime return.

And you'll well and truly be the right kind of hero.

– *Financial Advisor*, January 2003

Q&A: A REALITY CHECK ON JUNK BONDS

Q: *Do you think that adding a small percentage of high-yield bonds to a growth portfolio makes any sense? I've heard arguments that it could actually increase the returns of an all-equity portfolio.*

A: High-yield debt is best understood not as junk bonds but as a sort of secured equity. (Or, if you prefer, not as low-grade bonds but as high-grade stock.) Thus, junk bonds – the appellation I prefer to the psychologically palliative "high-yield" – should (and do) have return and volatility characteristics somewhere between those of debt and equity, and closer to equity.

The longshoreman philosopher Eric Hoffer said that to the child and the stockbroker all things are possible. But even he – and certainly I – would have to marvel at the notion that adding any kind of debt to an equity portfolio would raise the overall return of the portfolio. This would well and truly be alchemy. What you *may* have heard someone (probably a junk bond fund wholesaler) say is something to the effect that adding junk debt to an equity portfolio increases the *risk-adjusted* rate of return of the portfolio, in that it lowers the return a little but allegedly lowers the volatility a little more. This allegation may even be true, in some cold, intellectual way that has nothing to do with how real people really react to volatility. But it makes my eyes glaze over.

If you're looking for the returns of equities, stick to equities.

– *NMI*, January 2003

TO EVERYTHING THERE IS A SEASON

I'm deeply suspicious of alleged patterns in financial market behavior. In particular, it seems to me that market anomalies which show up consistently for a while are the engines of their own destruction. That's because when enough people spot the pattern, and begin sending tidal waves of money toward it, the anomaly drowns. (This explains (a) why all hedge funds blow up and (b) the spectacular meltdown of the "Dogs of the Dow" theory a few years back.)

All of that said, I find it hard to ignore this chart of average returns for the DJIA over the four years of the presidential election cycle for the last hundred years.

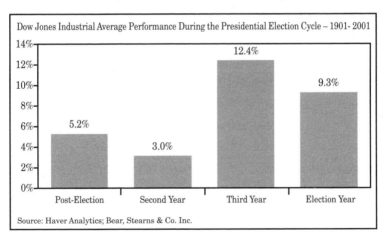

Dow Jones Industrial Average Performance During the Presidential Election Cycle – 1901- 2001

Source: Haver Analytics; Bear, Stearns & Co. Inc.

I take comfort from the fact that there is some not inconsiderable fiscal logic to this pattern. To wit, there's historically been a significant likelihood of increased federal spending and/or tax cuts in the third year (i.e. the pre-election year) of the cycle. Conversely, the tough/expensive/unpopular fiscal decisions tend to get made in the early years of the cycle, in the hope that they'll be forgotten by the next election.

If logic governs markets (and that's a gigantic "if"), this pattern could have considerable relevance in 2003, and perhaps on into 2004. Because unless the economy goes on a roaring reflationary tear very soon – which, though improbable, is very far from impossible – we are almost certainly going to get some kind of tax cut/fiscal stimulus legislation this year.

The president and his party can be expected to seek a legitimately pro-growth bill, which may involve accelerating the marginal rate cuts in the 2001 legislation, making estate tax repeal permanent and/or mitigating if not abolishing the double taxation of dividends. The minority party will demagogue this from here 'til Tuesday week as a boondoggle for the rich, and go for its usual sunshower-on-the-Gobi-desert cash-back scheme for, and I quote, "working families." (Note to Senator Daschle: my family earns – and pays taxes on – a seven figure income. Want to know how? *We work our tails off.*)

But I digress. My point is that, however the tax relief/ stimulus legislation sorts out, legislation – in this third year of the cycle – there will almost surely be. (If you doubt this, you still don't know George W. Bush, who is widely believed to have gone to Washington to finish his father's work, *and in fact went there to finish Ronald Reagan's.*)

That being the case, don't be too quick to laugh this chart off, because this year it's got about as much wind at its back as I can ever remember. A tax-cutting president with a Congressional majority and an economy appearing to recover much more slowly than people want it to are only part of the story. Remember that the stock market went down three years in a row from 2000 through 2002.

In all the hundred years of this chart, it's only gone down for a fourth year once, in 1932.

– *NMI*, January 2003

THREE IDEAS ABOUT CHANGE

You must become the change
you want to see in the world.
— Gandhi

Stop talking about what the good person should be,
and just be that person.
— Marcus Aurelius

It changes when you change.
— Dr. Betty Shabazz

2002'S TOP TEN BOOKS FOR ADVISORS

It's axiomatic that advisors suffer from massive information overload. Less obvious but even more important is that it's largely the wrong kind of information.

Most of what advisors see is focused on markets and the economy in the near term, and thus it distills (or simply retails) whatever issues are currently in the news. This phenomenon makes advisors two things they should never be: predictive and reactive, changing outlooks (and portfolios) far too often, either because of something the economy/market just did, or something it's alleged to be just about to do.

We crave perspective, and a framework for looking at the financial world that helps us recognize and deal appropriately with current trends in a larger, better context. The ephemera of the moment show up in magazines, research reports and market commentary, but real perspective, for me, is still found in books.

Ten books appeared in 2002 which, taken together, will make even very experienced advisors doubly effective – or at least twice as comfortable with their understanding of the economy, the capital markets and the business of advice. In no particular order, they were:

1. *Triumph of the Optimists*, by Elroy Dimson, Paul Marsh and Mike Staunton. This is Jeremy Siegel

on a grand scale, in that it traces the returns of the various asset classes in 16 developed countries from 1900 through 2000, looking for a consistent pattern – and finding one. For those who fear that the great superiority of equity vs. debt returns in the U.S. (as documented by Siegel, and by Ibbotson) is somehow a fluke, or a passing fancy, *Triumph* is a magnificent hymn to the universality of the equity risk premium. We all know that this *time* isn't different; *Triumph* proves that this *place* isn't different. The superior performance of equities is a force of nature.

2. *Dot.con: The Greatest Story Ever Sold*, by John Cassidy. This is both the definitive history of the Internet (from its earliest beginnings, in the mind of FDR's science advisor Vannevar Bush, in 1945) and the most complete account we're ever likely to get of the great financial bubble and crash which the Internet spawned. Read *Dot.con* for its peerless reportage, and skip Cassidy's dumb, declinist conclusions.

3. *It's Getting Better All The Time: 100 Greatest Trends of the Last 100 Years*, by Stephen Moore and Julian Simon. I may be cheating a little on this one, because I'm not sure it was published in 2002; I just found out about it recently. Amid today's popular pessimism, this book is a dispassionate (and accessibly anecdotal) recitation of the

huge progress in every area of human life – from lengthening life expectancies to falling infant mortality rates to soaring per capita income to the cratering cost of computing and communication. In particular, some of the statistical snapshots of improvements in the environment are wonderfully, counterintuitively startling. With just a few pithy paragraphs and a chart or two on each of the trends, this book is enormously readable. And at just $15, it's a great gift for better clients.

4. *The Force of Finance: Triumph of the Capital Markets*, by Reuven Brenner. A series of bite-sized, easily digestible essays, the general theme of which is that the economic success of some countries and the failure of others can be traced to the freedom, depth and transparency of their financial markets – or the absence thereof. Technical know-how is never the issue, for Brenner (else the Industrial Revolution would have happened in China); rather, the *financing* of know-how is the critical variable. This book ought to be an eye-opener for investment advisors, who may tend to forget that liquefying existing securities is actually the less important of the capital markets' two main functions.

5. *Free Trade Under Fire*, by Douglas A. Irwin. The greatest decade for economic freedom in human history – 10 years which saw the apotheosis of free markets and free trade in a globalizing world –

began with Ross Perot railing against the illusory "giant sucking sound" of U.S. jobs being lost to NAFTA, and ended with the Battle of Seattle, protesting the WTO's promotion of free trade. The supreme economic irony of our time is that, even as globalizing economic freedom lifted whole nations out of poverty, and as the world's standard of living made an unprecedented leap forward, fear and loathing of globalization both deepened and hardened.

Good advisors need to stand up for free trade and against protectionism among their clients and in their communities. They'll find Douglas Irwin's book the clearest, shortest, most compelling, least polemical defense of free trade that's yet been written. One by one, Irwin sets out all the arguments against free trade (e.g. "protecting American jobs"), and rationally demolishes them. If his exposition is at times dry, it's because he's trying so hard *not* to be a polemicist, and to let the clearly documented net benefits of globalization speak for themselves. This book will make you a better advisor and a more valuable citizen.

6. *Against The Dead Hand*, by Brink Lindsey. Another look at issues surrounding the free-market, free-trade imperative. Lindsey thinks progress in this area is anything but inevitable, and that the collectivist impulse toward centralized,

planned national economies – no matter how badly discredited – is far from dead. We've recently seen a mad rush to re-regulate the securities markets. And, rather than trying to get the FBI and the CIA talking to each other, our response to terrorism was to create a huge new federal bureaucracy, the Department of Homeland Security. However anecdotally, these developments tell you that the instinct for big government hasn't gone away, and make Lindsey's book an important cautionary read.

7. *Rainbow's End: The Crash of 1929*, by Maury Klein. Market history in popular form at its very best, and the most intriguing account of the greatest bubble and crash *until this one* to be published in a long time. As we sift through the wreckage of the tech/telecom/dot.com fiasco, this book offers useful perspective on the timelessness and persistence of "new era" financial fantasies – and their inevitably terrible ends. Moreover, it's fun to read.

8. *The Joy of Freedom: An Economist's Odyssey*, by David R. Henderson. Henderson, a Canadian, started out as a math major/physics minor in college, but fell in love with economics (or, more accurately, with freedom). This book is both his story and his belief system: wholly devoid of abstruse mathematics, it's almost an economics course for non-economists, and therefore potentially very

helpful to the busy advisor. Most of us come to capitalism for the efficiency and stay for the morality, but David Henderson's odyssey was in the opposite direction. Fascinating and (really!) entertaining.

9. *Who's Afraid of Adam Smith? How the Market Got Its Soul*, by Peter J. Dougherty. I had a ball reading this book, and it salved my conscience at never actually having read Smith. Dougherty, a veteran editor of economics books, is (like Henderson, above) deeply interested in Smith's view of capitalism not as some pitiless Darwinian law of the jungle but as a moral (as well as economic) force. Advisors should love the marketplace, not just respect it, and this delightful book will help you do both.

10. *Building a World-Class Financial Services Business: How To Transform Your Sales Practice into a Company Worth Millions*, by Don Schreiber, Jr. The only "how-to" book on this list, and deservedly so. Many advisors struggle to create business plans and client service platforms, as well as practices that have real value to a potential buyer. However dryly, Schreiber provides deep, detailed, authoritative and very credible solutions to these common, vexing organizational issues.

– *Financial Advisor*, February 2003

THE YEAR OF EYE CONTACT

Great professionals in every calling are great for a lot of similar reasons. One, of course, is a passion for what they do – a love of practicing their craft, and of the benefits their clients receive from it.

Another hallmark of greatness is the ability to identify the critical issue or task, and to focus single-mindedly on it. I don't think it's merely an ability to prioritize; that makes one good, but not necessarily great. Rather, it's the genius for seeing the one "mission critical" variable, and the discipline of not getting sidetracked.

The next generation of great financial advisors will look back at the year 2003 as a turning point in their careers. And I'm convinced they'll agree: the critical variable was eye contact.

In this resource, as well as in my recent *Financial Advisor* columns and speaking engagements, I've maintained that we advisors find ourselves in extraordinarily favorable circumstances – which are far too good to last.

Demographically, the first great wave of baby boomers is entering its mid-fifties, and feeling the maximum urgency to face the realities of pre-retirement planning. Moreover, they're not the smug do-it-yourselfers of five years ago. They don't just need advice, they *know* they need it. So, too, do their parents: the startlingly affluent children of the Depression, just now about to begin bequeathing some $10 trillion over the next decade or so. *This is the golden age of financial planning.*

Cyclically, we're slowly emerging from the wreckage of the greatest financial bubble and crash of our lifetimes, if not *anyone's* lifetime. For only the fifth time in 100 years, the broad stock market declined nearly 50%. After the last time it did that, in 1973-74, the equity market proceeded to go up 20 times in the next 25 years – not counting dividends. *The advisor who's joyously pounding that (long-term) table now will save the boomers and inherit the earth.*

But every silver lining has a cloud, and the current situation, though uniquely replete with opportunities, has its own set of difficulties which must be overcome.

First of all, coming out of a once-in-a-generation bear market, investors' faith and confidence (such as they ever were) are terribly shaken, and they see potential disaster lurking everywhere. For it is an axiom of investor psychology that when perceived risk is highest, real risk is lowest, and vice versa.

Beyond that, though, is the public's fashionably shattered belief in the objectivity and trustworthiness of the advisor function itself. Although this appears to be unique to the current Adventures in Spitzerland, it's really as common as dirt. After every crash, there's a new set of villains to whom we can pin the list of our own sins, and then send off into the desert to die. Given a choice between concluding, "I speculated foolishly" or "I was defrauded," Americans will always opt for the latter, and the honest surviving advisor will have to bear the brunt.

The weapons we must use to slay these dragons are not charts and graphs, but faith and trust. And our experience tells us that these qualities can best (indeed, only) be communicated eye-to-eye.

Prospecting for the expansion of existing relationships and – far more importantly – the establishment of new ones is, for all the reasons cited so far, the single "mission critical" variable in today's opportunity-rich environment. *And the success of that effort will be a pure and absolute function of the amount of quality face time you cause to happen in 2003.*

These truths may dictate some difficult choices. If you were planning to devote, say, 80 hours this year (of the roughly 1600 working hours you've maximally got to spend) to the CFP course, or 100 hours to analyzing and comparing money managers, you may want to give those budgets some more thought.

I'm not suggesting that these and all similar pursuits are objectively bad uses of your time. (For the record, the CFP course is a great investment of time, and managing managers an almost total waste of it.) I'm calling the question: at this golden moment – with our professional sun, moon and stars aligned as they've never been before and won't ever be again – *what is the very best use of your time?* I think we must conclude that, for the duration, face time is the best time.

Mediocrity can often do a number of things fairly well. Excellence does one optimal thing greatly. Choose. There's not a moment to lose.

– *NMI*, February 2003

Q&A: RE-SETTING THE FEE AGENDA

Q: *I heard you say long ago that your fee is only an issue when your value is in question. I completely agree – and whenever it is an issue, I know I must reflect on why, so that I can improve on how I work with and serve my clients. That being said, I have a client couple who are retiring. The husband is getting a lump sum that would increase my assets under management nearly fourfold. He values our relationship and wants the money to come to me. But the wife is having a hard time dealing with the fact that they will now be paying me $12,000+ per year. The husband asked me to enlighten the wife about the risks of managing this money without advice. I would also appreciate your ideas about how to respond.*

A: By repeating the dollar amount of the fee rather than the percentage, you are (unconsciously, I think) ceding the agenda to her, and if you do that you're going to lose. My interrogatory way of explaining the fee appears on pps. 232-235 of *The New Financial Advisor*. (In substantially the same form, it appears as "Q&A: Explaining Fees" on page 83 of this book.) I urge you to stay very close to this verbiage, which (among other things) relentlessly quotes the fee as a percentage of the assets: the minuscule one percent. Two cautionary procedural tips: (1) Do not, under any circumstances, make this statement to him alone. She isn't listening to him (nor, I suspect, to you, but there's only one way to find out). Explain the fee to both or neither. *If you are not looking right into her eyes when you do this, I guarantee you're going to lose.* (2) If, after you make the one percent statement, *she says the dollar amount even one more time,* you can assume it's over. Very politely thank them for their time, tell them you'll be happy to guide them on the terms you've described, invite them to inform you of their decision at their convenience, and leave.

– *NMI*, February 2003

IRAQ AND THE MARKET:
AN INQUIRY INTO THE NATURE
OF UNCERTAINTY

As this is written, in mid-January 2003, there seems a growing likelihood that the United States will lead an armed incursion into Iraq within a few months.

We appear already to have crossed the Rubicon. Indeed, as Fouad Ajami writes in the current issue of *Foreign Affairs*, "Any fallout of war is certain to be dwarfed by the terrible consequences of America's walking right up to the edge of war and then stepping back, letting the Iraqi dictator work out the terms of another reprieve."

But the purpose of this essay is neither to predict nor to advocate for military intervention in Iraq. It is to inquire, on behalf of our advisor/subscribers and their clients, into the chilling investment uncertainty which must surround the runup to such an event. And to see what if any light the historical record can shine through that fog. For, as Churchill said, the further we look back, the further we may see ahead.

In 1990, when Saddam Hussein occupied Kuwait, the U.S. and its allies rapidly deployed half a million troops in the Gulf, and called upon him to withdraw. He refused, promising "the mother of all battles."

There was good reason to take him seriously. His was the

army which had fought the Iranians to a bloody stand-still over eight years, cheerfully accepting hundreds of thousands of casualties in the process. He would be fighting close to home and on very familiar ground, in stark contrast to our forces. Finally, he was and is a Hitlerian madman, almost certainly willing, *in extremis*, to take his whole country (if not the world) down with him.

These and many other potential adversities were well – indeed, exhaustively – retailed in the press and on the talk shows. The spurious analogy to Vietnam was heard in every quarter. And anyone who was an advisor in those days will remember the total paralysis that descended upon the investing public as the January deadline we'd given Saddam drew ever nearer.

In the event, the "war" consisted of 38 days of massive bombing, followed up by four (count 'em: four) days of ground action.

Nor can I forebear to say something about the market backdrop to these events. Oil had peaked, and the market troughed, on the same day: October 11, 1990, at $40.42 a barrel and 295 on the S&P 500 – the latter a 16% decline since August 2, when Saddam's tanks rolled. When the allied attack began on January 20, 1991, oil collapsed and the stock market rallied sharply. By July, oil had halved to $21 and the S&P 500 had hit 380, up 29% from the trough. Granting that no economic/market analogy is perfect, I think these data may be suggestive.

More recently, in 2001, the U.S. acted to depose the Taliban regime in Afghanistan – the country which had been the USSR's ten-year Vietnam. Once again, the possibility (or, as some pundits had it, the probability) of a quagmire was endlessly debated.

The bombing campaign began on October 7. Three weeks later, on October 31, when the bombardment wasn't producing instant results, R.W. Apple, Jr. of the *New York Times* actually wrote, "Could Afghanistan become another Vietnam?" And, while acknowledging that this question "may be" premature, he intoned that it wasn't unreasonable.

In fact, it was ludicrous. By November 15, Afghanistan had been cut in half, with our allies in control of the north; Kabul had fallen. On December 7, Kandahar fell, and the Northern Alliance, its Pashtun allies and the U.S. controlled the whole country. "In all," Bob Woodward reports in his new book *Bush At War*, "the U.S. commitment to overthrow the Taliban had been about 100 CIA officers and 316 Special Forces personnel, plus massive airpower."

And, although the idea of the financial markets as a one-variable equation in those chaotic weeks is even more silly than usual, let the facts speak for themselves. The S&P 500 was around 1060 when the first bombs fell. It rallied immediately to 1100, then fell back to 1060 on Apple day (October 31) amid the growing quagmire noise. Then, as events cascaded in our favor, it ran to a high of 1170, finishing at 1160 on December 7.

I caution you against trying to read too much into these market data. The 1990 lows were never seen again, but the rally in late 2001 died, and the market crashed to new lows the following year.

Nor is any war exactly analogous to any other. I seek only to suggest three general points which may help you help your clients make better decisions than they otherwise might under the onslaught of journalism's relentlessly negative groupthink. To wit:

1. The U.S. has gone into not entirely dissimilar situations in recent years with force that brings new meaning to the word "overwhelming." It has subdued in weeks countries which mighty enemies could not vanquish in years, *including the foe it now faces.*
2. The markets have tended to rise in anticipation of, or on the commencement of, actual combat, and to rise further on its successful conclusion.
3. Winning a war can't *keep* markets up – only a healthy, growing economy can do that. But staying out of markets in order to assess a war's progress has not, since Vietnam, been a successful investment strategy.

The absence of job growth excepted, war jitters are about the last horse a pessimist can ride these days. And if post-

Cold War history is any guide, that horse may be quite literally about to get shot out from under him.

– *NMI*, February 2003

WHY ARE YOU MANAGING MANAGERS?

I recently spoke at a large conference of the agents of an excellent life insurance company, and was preceded to the podium by one of this company's more successful practitioners.

In about 45 minutes – without fanfare, histrionics or much of anything but the bare facts – this guy described what I thought was just about the perfect practice. From financial planning philosophy through staffing practices and down to china cups for the clients' coffee, he had me nodding so often and so hard I about snapped my neck. By the time I followed him to the stage – after his thunderous standing O – I was almost (but not quite) literally speechless. (Note to self: don't let them trick you into following that so-and-so *ever again*.)

I was most impressed – and that's saying something – by what this traditional life guy (25 years in the business, straight out of college) had to say about his practice's asset gathering/portfolio management activities. Or perhaps, more properly, by what he didn't say. Because this agent was totally silent on any number of issues which many readers of this magazine consider life-and-death.

- **He didn't say whether they used active management, indexing, or both.** I could be wrong, but I don't think he *forgot* to talk about this. (He was extremely well-organized, and was working from what I believe is called a Power Point presentation.) So either I missed this, or he didn't think it was important enough to comment on. At least, *not as important as china cups*, if you take my none-too-subtle point.

- **He didn't say what managers/mutual funds/ sub-accounts they used.** Instead he seemed fixated – poor simple soul that he is – on asset allocation. Said it was where the huge preponderance of your lifetime return comes from, and that it was about the only investment variable they seemed able to control.

Said the long-term return of stocks was about 11%, and that of bonds six percent, so that if you went 60%/40% equity/debt you should end up with about nine percent, or 80% of the return of stocks, with a heck of a lot less volatility. (That's how enthralled I was by this guy: I let that pass.)

- **He didn't express an economic or market outlook.** By this time, I was starting to have a pretty good handle on how the guy's mind works. So, although I can't prove this to you, I'm going to go out on a limb, here, and tell you what I believe. *He didn't express an outlook because he didn't have one*, and he didn't have an outlook because he didn't need one. It would be irrelevant to his fundamental asset allocation approach. And it might even be wrong.

Now, dear reader, the larger your professional and emotional investment in these three variables, the more readily you'll be inclined to conclude that, over the last year, this practice must have brought in $16.28 in new investment money. Wrong again, of course: they are gathering assets on an unprecedented, and accelerating, scale.

What, then, is the appeal? What is the pitch? What does this life insurance agent, who by his own admission needs a staffer to do the account-opening paperwork when he wins new investment business, say to people? As it turns out, he says just what he's been saying for 25 years:

- **Your investment decisions, like all your other financial decisions, should be driven by your long-term goals.** You'll either die or retire. If you die, you'll have life insurance. If you retire, you'll have investments. Now, how much retirement income will you need; what returns do you need to get in the interim in order to endow that income; what asset mix would it take, at historical returns, to get you where you need to go while still preserving your ability to get at least some sleep most nights? (There's a name for this thought process, and it's not portfolio management. It's financial planning.)

- **You'll consistently get the best return with the least effort/grief if you key on asset allocation.** As distinctly opposed to what we allegedly sophisticated investment advisors obsess about: selection and timing.

- **Having put almost all your effort into the variable that controls almost all your return, walk away.** Get your fun and/or your romance and/or your adrenaline rushes somewhere else. Don't get euphoric, don't get panicky and, when you're *really* ready to grow up, don't read your statements.

- **Don't manage your managers.** You either think you can fly a plane better than professional pilots can (and, moreover, have the time and energy to do so), or you don't. If you do, don't hire pilots: it's a waste of money, and their relative incompetence will just upset you. If you don't, hire professional pilots. Then, all you have to do is *stay the hell out of the cockpit*.

- **You hire an advisor not to manage money but to manage you.** You're only human: sooner or later you're going to try to slip into the cockpit. But you have no business in there, and anything you do in there will ultimately detract from rather than adding to the safety and efficiency of the flight. *You pay an advisor to keep you from entering the cockpit.* Even – and especially – when Lou Dobbs, or

Robert Prechter, or your whole bridge club assures you you're flying straight into a typhoon.

- **Relax. You'll live longer. And happier. You pay an advisor, and a team of portfolio managers, to worry so you don't have to.** It's going to be a long flight. Try to get some sleep. We'll wake you up when we get there.

The speaker then regaled us with a couple of stories about the kind of rubes who would fall for a come-on like that.

One was his brother, who is immensely successful at...I don't remember what, but he was sure he could manage his own investments better than this "Portfolio Management in Monosyllabic Words for Pre-School Children" approach. The agent said, "Let's halve the money for a year and test your theory." The brother brought in his half five months later.

Another yokel was making $5 million a year running a company, and trading stocks on the side. The agent, who'd gone in there to do an estate plan, was simply appalled. "Are you making any money doing this?" "Not really." "Are you having any fun?" "Not any more."

"How much more money would you make if you put that time and energy into your company?" the agent asked. "I shudder to think," the tycoon answered, and signed the transfer papers. And I, for one, will bet you that the broker who lost the trading account still has no idea what hit him.

I spent the first 15 years of my career being a person – and watching other people – who tried to be very good at both gathering assets *and* managing investments. I found that one might do either, but that no one could do both.

Words cannot express my delight, therefore, when at the end of the 1980s the whole world began migrating from individual stocks and bonds to mutual funds. Transported by joy, I sat down and knocked out a book called *Serious Money*, which looked forward to a halcyon era when professional management would free up 50% (and more) of our time, and let us work only on what we could really be good at, which was and is asset gathering and behavior modification.

A dozen years later still, I find far too many advisors squandering 50% (and more) of their time...*managing managers*.

That's exactly the wrong answer. And wouldn't it be ironic if it's the life insurance industry – and not the investment professionals at all – who've figured that out?

– *Financial Advisor*, March 2003

THE MORAL AND INTELLECTUAL
BANKRUPTCY OF MARKETING
DIRECTLY TO THE INVESTOR

During January 2003, in newspapers and magazines across the country, a very well-known money management firm – which markets primarily though not at all exclusively to the do-it-yourself investor – was running a full-page advertisement.

The ad was for about a half-dozen of this firm's funds – all bond funds – and its primary feature was a box showing how many Morningstar stars each fund had earned over various periods of time.

This is not the most evil ad I've ever seen. That distinction belongs to Charles Schwab's "Let's put some lipstick on this pig," in which a brokerage sales manager urges his salespeople to commit securities fraud. (Knowing that it has no credible record of offering investors personal advice – fee-based or otherwise – Schwab simply elected to finger-point, in the most distasteful way, at commissioned advisors. The message: we may not, to the discerning eye, have any demonstrable competence, so let's call the competition felons. This is the act of a firm that has completely lost its way, and is beginning to make heart-stoppingly bad decisions.)

But the star-crossed bond fund ad is, I think, the final declaration by a leader in the direct marketing of investments of the complete moral and intellectual bankruptcy of that business model.

For it is not simply wrong to be pounding the table for bond funds at this point in the cycle; it is morally reprehensible. (1) We are clearly at or near the bottom of a secular interest rate cycle, so that, with any sustained recovery/reflation, interest rates will rise and bond prices fall. (2) Even worse, the yield curve has steepened considerably. And a tremendous amount of intermediate-to-longer-term debt is held by entities who borrowed short to finance those purchases, and are living on the spread. As in 1994, when the yield on the long Treasury bond shot up 50% in under six months, any significant backup in rates may cause these positions to be unwound in a stampede out of longer-term paper. Thus, the next 30% market decline is at least as likely to happen in bonds as it is in stocks – maybe much likelier.

But a direct marketer can't *say* those things. Indeed, it can't say anything that a patient, empathetic, caring advisor can say, *because it isn't an advisor.* It's a marketer, perpetually renting investor money by serially telling the *lumpenproletariat* whatever it most wants to hear at any given moment. This is my definition of moral bankruptcy.

Intellectual bankruptcy is implicit in the ad's use of the most thoroughly discredited rating system in the history of mutual funds, if not in the whole history of investing: the Morningstar star system. As Morningstar has had the good grace to acknowledge (see page 142 of this book), buying five-star funds and shunning one-star funds has been, over many years, a foolproof strategy for the most appalling underperformance. But instead of retiring this whole terribly flawed, ultimately misleading approach, it has simply "revised" its methodology – as if, for all the world, that's going to make any difference. And the direct marketers simply plug in the new (i.e. untested) star system, confident that the mob doesn't even know that this is an issue.

We live in a moment when even the best advisors are bitterly second-guessing themselves, wondering how we could have been so wrong about any number of aspects of the market over the last few years. And it's right that we do so, first of all because we should accept our responsibility, and also because mistakes are, ultimately, the way most of us learn.

But an ad for four- and five-star bond funds should help us keep our own shortcomings in some kind of proper perspective. We may have been wrong – indeed, very wrong. And being human, we may yet be wrong again.

But we're not stupid. And we're not evil. Do-it-yourself is both – not so much because it wants to be as because it *has* to be.

– *NMI*, March 2003

Q&A: JUST SAY NO
TO DOLLAR-COST AVERAGING LUMP SUMS

Q: *I have a client whose husband passed away and who received life insurance proceeds of $2 million. She is 37 and has three children under the age of six. She needs approximately $100,000 per year in income. Should a portion of the money be set aside to cover her income needs for the next two to three years, with the rest invested in a diversified stock portfolio to be drawn on three years from now? Should the money be dollar-cost averaged or fully invested right away?*

A: All of the money should be invested immediately repeat immediately in a diversified portfolio of managed equity accounts from which she can withdraw five percent per year to cover her income needs. Dollar cost averaging lump sums is always a sucker bet, but doing so after three straight down years in the stock market (when there's only been one fourth straight down year in the last century) is, at least statistically, criminal.

– *NMI*, March 2003

Q&A: ON ASSET ALLOCATION IN 529 PLANS

Q: *Regarding 529 plans: could you please give me some insight as to what the weightings should be in equities for people who have children in their early teens? Many plans offer age-based portfolios (equities to fixed income), but I was wondering if you had a view that may differ.*

A: I've always used as a rule of thumb that capital which would be needed in less than five years should consider staying out of equities, because the volatility of returns over periods so short is not something to be laughed off. So, for instance, a 13-year-old, who'll need college money more or less evenly in four, five, six and seven years, would be roughly half in equities (for the last two years of tuition) and half in debt (for the first two).

The facts that you're coming off the deepest bear market in equities in nearly 30 years, and are looking at the lowest interest rates in 40 years, might tend to make one skew more heavily toward equities over those next four to eight years. Then again, they might not, depending on the clients' psychology. But I think that as the economy recovers in this decade, both corporate earnings and interest rates will firm. This is relatively good for equities and relatively bad for bonds. Bottom line: I'd sit down with the family, lay this all out for them, and let their hearts be the asset allocator. Education is (and ought to be) a very emotional issue with many people, and a four-to-eight year window (or less) is too short for you to be able to really pound the table either way.

– *NMI*, March 2003

TUITION AT 40

The senior editor of *Nick Murray Interactive*, a Cameron Crazy of long standing, recently informed me that tuition, room and board at her alma mater would be $40,000 for the coming academic year. Duke thus joins the growing ranks of highly selective private colleges whose costs have hit that big round number.

Ironically, though, it is not private but state schools at which costs are rising the fastest, as strapped states back away from their schools as rapidly as politically possible. The state universities of Connecticut and Maryland have already posted nine percent increases for next year. But the venerable commonwealth of Taxachusetts, with an eye-popping 24% bump, may already be a shoo-in for this year's stop-Dad's-heart sweepstakes winner.

The thing about college costs is that you could never – least of all now – *save* for them. Because long before today's breakaway increases, costs were rising faster than any rates of return you could ever reasonably expect to get on savings. Rather, you have to *invest* for college – and, if at all possible, invest on a tax-protected basis, because that's the real way to gain ground on cost increases. In that sense, 529 plans, as souped up by the 2001 tax legislation, are manna from heaven.

The key to 529, of course, is the ability to put away a lot of money in a hurry, and not trigger a gift tax. Which tells you who the ultimate 529 market is: not the kids' parents, who probably don't have a lot of money to invest regardless of how nifty the tax break, but the *grandparents*.

This may seem intuitively obvious to advisors as smart as the subscribers to this resource clearly are. If so, I apologize for taking up your valuable time. But if not – or just: if you're not pounding away at this issue in your seminars and prospecting – you may want to think this through one more time.

Because 529 instantly makes you a multigenerational advisor to a family. And in a business where as little as 15% of invested dollars stay with the average advisor when the first client generation dies, anything that keeps you serving a family across the generations becomes a critical career tool.

– *NMI*, March 2003

Q&A: EVALUATING YOUR OPTIONS IN
DEPLETED SYSTEMATIC WITHDRAWAL PLANS

Q: *I have retired clients in their late fifties whose withdrawal rates on their portfolios have gotten high as a result of the downturn in the market. Several have asked me if I think they will need to return to work at some point. They have all pretty much said the same thing, which is that they would rather return to work now (while they are still relatively young) instead of later. I am unsure of what advice to give these people.*

A: So am I, so I think the best thing to do is just lay out their options, which, as I see them, are any or all of (a) toughing it out, (b) cutting back or eliminating the withdrawal, (c) working now, (d) working later, and/ or (e) taking a home equity loan for the next year or two's living expenses, meanwhile turning off the withdrawals.

– *NMI*, March 2003

ARE YOU MANAGING YOUR CLIENTS OR LEADING THEM?

"An army of deer led by a lion
will defeat an army of lions led by a deer."

– attributed to former NFL great Calvin Hill
by his son, current NBA great Grant Hill

Q&A: PRIORITIZING YOUR PRESENTATIONS

Q: *I take too much time in plan presentations. Meetings drag on, and I do way too much talking. Clients generally do everything I recommend, but instead of getting it all done in one to one-and-a-half hours, it can run two to three hours. How do you handle this when there is so much information to go over?*

A: There isn't that much information to go over; you're covering secondary and tertiary material, and in excessive detail, at that. No presentation should take more than 45-50 minutes unless the client is constantly breaking in, asking for more detail – in which case the meeting can take as long as it takes. I suggest you summarize everything in a format which would bring you home well within 40 minutes, tell the client up front that that's what you're doing, and invite him to ask for as much or as little more detail as he needs, but that you don't want to overload him. In general, I've always believed that the longer a presentation, the less well thought out it is, and the less effective it will be.

– *NMI*, March 2003

THE RISK SHIFTS TO THE UPSIDE

The more cable channels, Internet "news" services and magazines there are, the more they tend, at any given moment, to all be covering the same "story." This being the case, the only way they can compete with each other is to make their coverage more shrill and sensational than their competition. An all-too-depressing example was the non-stop drumbeat on all the New York City TV stations that said, "We're at Orange Alert for terrorist activity, but stay tuned: any minute now we may go/expect to go/will surely go to Red Alert." (Of course, we never did.)

So, as this is written in the third week of February 2003, the stock market waxes and wanes by the hour, driven by whatever blathering is going on at – of all places – the United Nations. And the one story of the day is "war" with Iraq...which replaced the *last* one and only story, the sluggishness in the labor market.

That one has seen both of these movies before – and indeed seen them as a double feature, though in reverse order, in 1990-91 – only adds to one's ennui and distraction. Does no one remember the utter pall that settled over the markets in late 1990, as Operation Desert Shield built to its anti-climax as the nonevent of the century? Does no one remember the media decrying layoffs, downsizing and "corporate killers" in 1991, even as the economy slowly gained the traction necessary to launch its longest sustained advance since the Depression? Does no one see that the media-crazed mob always isolates on the wrong variable, *and always reads that variable incorrectly* (viz. Y2K)?

Well, one does or one doesn't, and in the end it won't really matter: the mob is going to do whatever it's going to do, and if you follow the mob you must fail financially, just as the mob itself always does. That's not my point.

A massively complex (and fundamentally prosperous) economy like ours can never be reduced to one variable – other than on the shortest-term basis, and the short term is of interest only to speculators and traders. Rather, the economy and the markets which reflect it are a mass of conflicting currents, some salutary and others negative.

Thus, the intelligent investor and his advisor (if they watch the macroeconomy at all, which one devoutly hopes they don't) attempt to assess conditions *on balance*. The question is never whether the very last risk has gone away – it hasn't – but whether the preponderance of economic forces is decisively positive or negative. This, in turn, indicates whether the dominant investment risk lies in being in or out of the equity market.

This has nothing to do with predicting a bottom. Indeed, there are very few guarantees in this life, but one is that *you are going to miss the bottom.* You do, however, get to choose how you'll miss it: either by being early and absorbing some more temporary declines so as to lose none of the coming upsurge, or by being late, and paying up (perhaps way up) for "certainty." Simply put, at any given moment you have to decide whether the greater risk lies in being in the equity market or being out of it. (The truly great long-term risk is *always* being out, but no one can handle that for the moment.)

Over the last two calendar quarters, I believe that the preponderant risk has shifted decidedly to the upside – that, much more than at any time in the last five years, the risk is being out of the equity market.

First, much of the Iraq-related uncertainty is probably about to get resolved. And it isn't war the market hates, it's uncertainty. Moreover, with that resolution (and with Venezuelan oil production ramping back up), the artificially high price of oil should come down; the seasonal fall-off in demand as a bitter winter ebbs should also be a positive here.

The reflationary signals coming from gold and industrial commodities tell us that monetary policy is as accommodative as it is likely to get. What we need now is fiscal stimulus, in the form of pro-growth (as opposed to pro-consumption) tax relief. Particularly if the president's popularity took a big bounce on the successful completion of armed conflict in Iraq, such a tax program would become much more likely to pass. And real GDP growth in 2003 – after last year's saw-toothed but very respectable 2.8% – could get as high as four percent with the right kind of tax stimulus.

Add to these the fundamental engines of expansion, which are intact: the entrepreneurial/small-business nature of our economy; 131 million employed workers earning, spending and saving; record low interest rates and inventory-to-sales ratios, recovering corporate profits...and a whole generation of PCs, bought in 1999 to ward off Y2K, now rapidly obsolescing and needing to be replaced.

Finally, there are two technical factors near and dear to my heart, having to do with asset allocation – or, more properly, with the fatal propensity of the mob to zig when it ought to zag.

The first is the staggering balances in money market funds. Today, there is a dollar in a money market fund for every four dollars of equity market capitalization – a historically unprecedented 25%. The great market bottoms of 1987 and 1990 occurred when this figure reached the 15% area, and you may infer from that what you will. I infer that this is a powder keg, and that – though I know not the day nor the hour – it may explode in the form of a buying panic.

The other, even more dramatic factor is the precipitous drop in the percentage of America's assets in equities.

Now, let me confess my biases: the last time this percentage spiked downward, at the end of 1990, I wrote a magazine column called "The Next Best Thing To A Buy Signal From God," whereupon the market went up for 10 years. So I hope I'm not just trying to recover some faded glory when I tell you: it's happening again, with a mighty vengeance.

Using Federal Reserve figures and its own estimates, Bear Stearns recently calculated the asset allocation of the dominant holders of U.S. equities: bank personal trusts, households, life insurance companies, mutual funds, other insurance companies, private pension, state and local government, and retirement funds.

Bear found that the equity allocation of these groups, after peaking near an all-time high 55% early in 2000, had fallen to 35% in recent months. Interestingly, the last time this percentage fell 20 points was in the unwinding of the last great stock-price bubble, between 1968 and 1974.

Be assured that all of this proves nothing – except that the mob is shunning equities as it has rarely (and by some measures never) done before. The more (and the longer) it does so, the more the risk shifts to the upside.

– *NMI*, March 2003

SELECTION AND TIMING:
GETTING OFF THE DRUGS

The first quarter of 2003 was a busy season for me in terms of speaking engagements. Of the four or five dozen dates I budgeted for this year, I've probably already done about 30.

I confess that I attributed this surge to a burning desire on the part of the firms who've hired me to get a fresh perspective, to leave the wreckage of the past few years behind them, and to make a new and healthier start. But time after time, as I sat listening to the speakers who preceded me, I could close my eyes and it was 1997 again: all anybody wanted to talk about was selection and timing.

Have we learned nothing? Does no one see that it was selection and timing (chasing performance, calling turns in the markets, straining to be "right," zigging and zagging ourselves to distraction) that got us into all this trouble to begin with?

Does no one realize that, of all the weapons in the advisor's arsenal, selection and timing are the two over which he has the least control, and which will end up accounting for the smallest part of a family's lifetime return? *Are we determined to shuffle mindlessly onto that god-awful roller coaster yet again – and to call that a career?* (And the time to ask ourselves that question is now, before the roller coaster pulls out – not at the top of the next screaming drop.)

To help you resolve these issues in your own life – to inspire you with the courage to just say no to the drugs of selection and timing – I am delighted to report the results of a breakthrough study of the sources of lifetime return. In my never-ending quest to serve the industry which has done so much for me and my family, I've devoted myself to finding the Rosetta stone of returns – the once-and-for-all true answer to the age-old question of where real people's real returns really come from.

Forget every densely mathematical academic study you've ever read: this here is the real deal. The numbers you're about to see are beyond authoritative: they're definitive. Why, friends, I'll even go so far as to say that these statistics are *irrefutable*. And I'd know, because I myself just now made them up.

(1) The presence or absence of a financial plan: 49.1268%. My study found that a startling 49.1268% (and you know that number's got to be right, on account of it's so precise) of a family's total lifetime return comes from the stark, simple existence of a formal, written, comprehensive financial, investment and estate plan...or the absence thereof. People who have plans know where they're going, and (see below) have a clear, long-term strategy for getting there. Put another way, people with a plan tend to be *acting* in pursuit of their goals. While those with no plan tend always to be *reacting* – to markets, economic factoids, war scares, anthrax mailgrams, and other ephemera which, perhaps as soon as tomorrow, will be yesterday's news.

(2) Asset allocation: 24.9212%. Comprehensive planning forces a family to think in terms of their financial needs over the entire balance of their lives, and on into those of the people they love and must leave behind in the world. Such perspective focuses the asset allocation decision quite wonderfully.

I do not know how long an armed conflict in Iraq may take, nor what a subsequent nation-building effort may cost. I know that my wife's and my joint life expectancy exceeds 30 years, and that we are determined to live independently as long as we can – and in dignity if and when we no longer can. History suggests that the cost of living may triple during our remaining lives.

I do not know when a meaningful upturn in business investment will occur in the United States, but I know that my granddaughter Rebecca Giovanna Dickerson will almost certainly start college on or about August 25, 2018, and that her brother William Carleton Dickerson will most probably do likewise two years later to the day. I believe that their higher educations could, at current rates of escalation, cost upwards of three quarters of a million dollars. My wife and I have chosen to be responsible for the accumulation (and/or bequest) of these monies – not because we think their parents won't be able to do it, but because our personal values are such that we refuse to book the risk.

It will come as no surprise, then, that all of our investment capital is going into equities of one or another kind. This is in no way a call on the market (which we devoutly hope remains on its keester for years, though that seems improbable); it is the only course open to us given our long-term goals. We are equity investors not because of a market (timing) viewpoint, nor even necessarily because we want to be, but because history suggests no alternative. In that sense, we didn't make the asset allocation decision: our goals – as expressed in our plan – made it for us.

(3) Behavior modification/Big Mistake prevention: 24.1011%. This is where the excellent advisor really earns her spurs – not to mention her one percent annual fee. Indeed, you could (but probably better not) give away your financial planning and asset allocation services, and still be worth multiples of what you cost, simply by helping clients fail to step on eight great behavioral land mines.

Devotees of selection and timing get hooked on those drugs because of one simple, threshold misperception: that the key determinant of return is which investments you own and when you own them. That is, they fatally believe that the critical variable is **investment performance**. It isn't, of course. The last key component of total lifetime return, at precisely 24.1011%, is **investor behavior**, with us advisors as the behavior modifier.

And the real beauty of this one is that once you've got the asset allocation decision made right, you don't even have to get people to do anything positive. You just have to prevent them from, uh, bleeping up. (The only way ever discovered by man to fail to achieve all your financial goals in an asset class that's been compounding at 10%-12% since Coolidge was in the White House is: you bleep up.)

The eight great behavioral boo-boos are:

(a) **Overdiversification.** People buy the hot fund of the year in their 401(k) 10 years running – and end up with the world's most expensive, least efficient index fund.

(b) **Underdiversification.** Chasing the hot dot on the scattergram until the music inevitably stops, and you find yourself without a chair.

(c) **Panic.** The end of the world is nigh; I'm going to cash.

(d) **Euphoria.** Or call it, as Barber and Odean do, overconfidence (and as cynics do: greed). By any name, it's the loss of an adult sense of principal risk – the conviction that the only risk is being outperformed by other people.

(e) **Leverage.** In practice, it magnifies mistakes far more (and far more often) than it does return.

(f) **Investing for yield instead of total return**, or taking too little risk to achieve your goals.

(g) **Speculating instead of investing**, and not seeing the difference. "I'm investing in the future of e-commerce," circa 1999. No, you were speculating on the success of a business model which had never shown a profit, by buying start-up companies which never did and (now) never will.

(h) Letting cost basis dictate investment decisions. At the top: "Can't diversify out of my big winner now; can't afford to pay the capital gains tax." At the bottom: "Can't rebalance now; can't afford to take the losses."

Avoid these mistakes – which, without an advisor, no American ever will – and nearly the whole balance of your lifetime return is in the bag. So let's review the bidding:

Planning	49.1268%
Asset Allocation	24.9212%
Behavior Modification	<u>24.1011%</u>
	98.1491%

And there you have it, friends: scientific proof (or: a demonstration no sillier than most of what passes for scientific proof in this business) that the remaining *1.8509% of a family's total lifetime return comes from selection and timing.* Unless, of course, it's even less than that, which I don't rule out.

Are you laughing? Well, that's good, I guess...up to a point. But I'll tell you something in deadly earnest: if advisors put as much time and energy into goals and plans as they do into selection and timing, they and their clients would be a lot richer and happier. And the world would be a better place.

It starts when you just say no.

— *Financial Advisor*, April 2003

Q&A: A GOOD REFERRAL SOURCE
IS NO REASON TO TAKE A BAD ACCOUNT

Q: *Got a referral – retired physician – from a truly great client. Had the interview. Prospect says he's also talking to another advisor; asks me to present again, to his wife. Meeting went well; they wanted to give me the whole account. A week later, they're going with the other advisor; reasons not offered. I wished them well. Yesterday he calls, announces that he has suffered a mild stroke, and that he now wants to give me $250K of the $1.5 million. I said yes, if this account had clear goals and I knew what the other guy was doing so there wouldn't be duplication. I rationalized that to say "no" might reflect badly on my great referral source. (I think this may be another way of saying, "I need the eggs.") Help.*

A: Let me preface my answer with two observations. (1) There is no kind way to respond to you, so I will strive for the minimum unkindness required. Which you'll understand and accept, I'm sure, because (2) you already know the answer.

This account has disaster written all over it in letters 10 feet high, and this guy has given you every signal that he is a flake at best and something far more ominous at worst. That said, you have helped make the situation as bad as it could possibly be by making, *at every single turning point*, the worst mistakes imaginable.

(1) If the wife is a decision-maker, why didn't you know that? Why did you present to him in the first place? He abused you, and you took it. Hint: I don't blame *him* for this. (2) When they first said they were going with you, then did an about face a week later, that was your perfect opportunity to go back to the referral source and say, "Thanks; they picked someone else," and get clear. Your failure to do this is inexplicable. (3) When the guy came back yet again, post-stroke, you had every opportunity to say, "No thanks; I think you made the right decision for both of us," and to warn your referral source that the guy was getting really erratic on you. You did neither. (4) You never, *ever*, **ever** take part of an account, as I have been at extreme pains to point out in *TNFA* (and on pages 110 and 143 of this book).

You have to get rid of this guy immediately after telling your referral source the plain, adult truth: that the guy was dangerously indecisive before the stroke, that the stroke sure doesn't seem to have helped any, and that you don't believe you can genuinely help the guy. Do it now. Do not mistake the foregoing for a suggestion.

– *NMI*, April 2003

WAITING FOR THE CATALYST

As this is written, on the eve of St. Patrick's Day 2003, the stock market has just had its best rally in many a month on the realization that an armed conflict in Iraq might actually be very short. (Specifically, CNN reported something to the effect that we were secretly talking to the Iraqi army about throwing in the towel as soon as the bell rings at the beginning of Round One.)

Now, nobody knows why the market does what it does on one given day. And the current market gets whipped around on huge mood swings, with or without a particular rumor, more than any I've ever seen in my soon-to-be 36 years in the business. But the idea that everybody just suddenly realized one day that this war might be very brief seems especially weird. (The Iraqi army might surrender almost immediately? No duh! *What the hell choice did you think Tommy Franks and a quarter million of America's very best professional warriors were going to give them?*)

What this episode *does* show us, however, is how desperately ready this wildly oversold market is for a catalyst – an event that breaks the evil spell, and sets off the buying panic the potential for which is so deeply embedded in the market's technical condition.

Two months ago in this resource, in a piece called "Iraq and the Market," I tried to remind readers as dispassionately as I could that the commencement of hostilities in Desert Storm and Afghanistan (a) produced favorable military resolutions almost infinitely more quickly than anyone could have hoped and (b) set off very significant relief rallies in the stock market. (Indeed, the closing prices the night before our last foray against Iraq in Desert Storm have, in the main, never been seen again.) These thoughts were offered not as a prediction, but as a way of suggesting that if the market were to go a lot lower on the actual outbreak of war, this time would have to be different. *Very* different.

Then last month, in "The Risk Shifts to the Upside," I opined that the balance of risks lay decisively, perhaps for the first time in five years, in being out of the equity market rather than being in it. I cited (1) a looming end to uncertainty in Iraq; (2) a potentially sharp decline in oil prices from such an eventuality, as well as from some normalization in Venezuela and the waning of a bitter winter; (3) the stubborn refusal of the unemployment picture to worsen considerably, even as it refuses to improve...yet; (4) continuing real GDP and earnings recovery; (5) reflation, and the gradual return of pricing power; (6) the potential for some meaningful pro-growth tax relief; (7) the gradual acceleration of the tech/PC replacement cycle, as the python finishes digesting the pig it swallowed whole in 1999 ahead of Y2K; and (8) the technical condition of the equity market, particularly with respect to the oceans of cash on the sidelines and a historic drop in the public's equity asset allocation.

That essay, too, was not meant to be predictive, *at least as respects timing*. It just said: the danger that you're going to miss the train is not declining, and it is no longer trending sideways. The danger of missing the train is high, and rising.

I mean now to complete what I hope you will see is one long, continuous thought. I want to take us to Defcon Two – or, in the currently more fashionable argot, to put us on Orange Alert.

Because the continuing deterioration in the equity market since I last wrote (from S&P 850 right back down into that 800 "support" area) brought on very significant improvements in virtually all the sentiment indicators. That is, market participants – public and professional alike – have exhibited huge upsurges in bearishness since the S&P fell away from its high around 930 in mid-January. And that kind of capitulation never fails to hasten a turn of some importance.

But what really rang my chimes was that incredibly violent rally on March 12th, on a rumor that was no more than plain common sense. (It's just that the mood, at that point, was so hysterically negative that *common sense came as a shock*.) Because that excellent rally, accompanied as one would ideally want it to be by sell-offs in both bonds and gold, whispers to me that just about everything is now in place for an important turn, and that we're all, whether we realize it or not, just waiting for the catalyst.

When there is no good news priced into the stock market, almost any seriously good news will set it off. Just as the bond market, now putting so much white powder of negativity up its nose that it's in full-on bubble mode, will be destroyed by any seriously good news. But that's a subject for the accompanying essay, "The Bond Bubble."

I don't know what the catalyst will be. (The percentage bet is oil, which dropped $10 a barrel in the first trading day of Desert Storm. But I don't have to bet: I can invest.) Still less, as I believe I've demonstrated to your complete satisfaction these 18 months past, do I have any idea when it's coming.

But all my years and all my experience are telling me that this market, even if it needs still more hysterical capitulation in order to be completely cleaned out, is just as totally mispriced as it was in the first quarter of 2000, and for exactly the opposite reasons. And just as the market turned three years ago, so will this one turn, with a vengeance, just when the largest number of market participants say – *if they have not already said* – **"This will never end."**

– *NMI*, April 2003

WHERE THE REAL RISK LIES:
THE BOND BUBBLE

The stock market dropped some 14% peak-to-trough in eight weeks starting in mid-January 2003 – about 10% off last year's close. But that latest leg down – albeit relatively minor in the context of the whole three-year bear – set off disproportionately incremental bearishness and capitulation.

Where did all that money go? Against all reason, logic and historical probabilities, it went into bonds. In the process, I believe the bond market has gone from merely overbought/overvalued to the status of a full-fledged bubble. When that bubble bursts, the great secular bull market in bonds which began in 1981-82 will end, not with a whimper but with a very big bang. And investors who perceived bonds as a safe, sane alternative to the horrors of the stock market will discover – too late, and the hard way – where the real risk lay.

The handwriting is already quite clearly on the wall. By mid-March, yields on the 10-year Treasury had fallen to 3.65%. Far more ominously, the real yield on 10-year TIPS (Treasury Inflation Protected Securities) dropped to 1.75%, down from 2.25% at the end of 2002, 3.25% a year ago – and 4.4% around the beginning of 2000.

A real yield of 1.75% on 10-year TIPS discounts real GDP growth in the U.S. economy well below two percent over much or all of the next 10 years. So the potential buyer would rationally ask – just as one might have reasonably asked of Nasdaq three years ago – "Is this market pricing in expectations which are realistic?" Now as then, the answer would be no. Consider:

(1) Non-farm productivity growth averaged four percent over the last year, and 2.7% over the last five years. Is it reasonable to forecast GDP growth far below the rate of growth of productivity?

(2) Average GDP growth over the last five quarters (after the sharp upward revision of 4Q02) was 2.9%. Most forecasts are still in the 3.0%-3.5% range for the full year 2003; tax cuts are a wild card on the upside.

(3) Investment spending on equipment and software is accelerating, having risen at an average 5.5% real rate over the last three quarters.

(4) The feedback loop of lower mortgage rates into re-financing and thence into consumer spending continues.

(5) Gold, commodities and the dollar continue to signal reflation, which will ultimately raise red flags at the Fed, whose 1.25% fed funds rate is oxygen for the bond bubble. (The real short-term interest rate in the U.S. cannot remain negative indefinitely.)

These phenomena taken together point to sustainable real growth not below two percent, but far above it. If this conclusion is correct, bond yields are too low – perhaps much too low. More to the point of this essay: if yields are too low, bond prices are too high. *Perhaps much too high.*

There are, moreover, technical factors in the bond market that don't bode well for bond prices. One is the fact that of the recent massive inflows which have driven some rates to Eisenhower-era levels, some incalculable but probably huge percentage never meant to be in bonds at all. *It is flight capital,* and it is flying out of equities. When the pressure on the equity market abates, this capital will begin to fly back. Should the pressure on the equity market abate suddenly pursuant to a major catalyst (see the accompanying essay), the negative effect on bond prices could be quite dramatic.

Secondly, and just as importantly, the yield curve remains very steep. This tells you that (just as in 1993, the last time the real short-term interest rate went negative for upwards of a year) the wiseguys are playing the spread: borrowing short to lend long. When (not if) they move to unwind those positions, the longer end of the bond market will get crushed *all out of proportion to fundamentals* as everybody tries to get out the same closing window at the same time. This, in turn, gives rise to that rare and terrifying event in the bond market, the precise technical term for which is **NO BIDS**. As Citigroup Asset Management's Joe Deane said recently in my presence, "It is infinitely easier to buy a hundred million bonds in a falling interest rate environment than it is to sell them into rising rates."

To see what this is going to look like, return with us now to those thrilling days of yesteryear, 1994.

First, a little background. The fed funds rate, which had been as high as eight percent as recently as July 13, 1990, bottomed out at three percent on September 4, 1992. And there it languished for 17 months to the day: on February 4, 1994, it was raised to 3.25%.

And there the dam broke. The rate went up, faster and faster, six more times by the following February 1, when it peaked at six percent.

The devastation in the longer end of the bond market blasted through *all* rate-sensitive instruments, equity as well as debt. The Shearson long government bond index (10 years plus) dropped 15% in 13 months, and government bond mutual funds went into net liquidation in mid-1994. Lower quality debt got savaged proportionately worse, and even the Dow Jones utility stock index went down 30%. There was nowhere to hide: it was a massacre of the innocents. Rarely has the safety-seeking bond investor walked into such a buzzsaw. *Until now.*

Friends, the one thing I want to be sure to avoid is to have you sitting there thinking, "The old guy is saying that that could happen again."

Not at all, gentle readers. I'm saying that it *will* happen again. The only issue is when.

– *NMI*, April 2003

INCHING OUT OF HARM'S WAY

My basic premises for this little essay are fairly simple –
but, then again, look who you're dealing with.

(1) Whether or not it's completely cleaned out, the
stock market is just as mispriced at S&P 800 as it
was at S&P 1500, for exactly the opposite reasons.

(2) The bond market, at 3.65% on the 10-year Treasury and a 1.75% real yield on the 10-year TIPS,
is in bubble mode, its expectations no more realistic than the stock market's were in 1Q2000.

(3) Perceived risk and real risk are always inversely
correlated. As I write, the great unwashed think
the stock market extremely risky in the short to
intermediate term, and the bond market extremely
safe.

(4) The truth is exactly the opposite. The risk/reward
relationship of equities is as favorable as it's been
since 1991, and before that 1981. (Even if valuations are only back to where they were in, say,
1994.)

(5) The bond market, meanwhile, is as overbought and
overvalued as it's been since the end of 1993, the
last time the real fed funds rate was negative, and
just before that rate about doubled in the next 12
months or so. If and to the extent that that's right,
the next 20% market decline won't be in stocks,
but bonds.

(6) Clients – and, even more importantly, prospects – are terribly underweighted in equities and overweighted in bonds.

(7) Clients – and, even more importantly, prospects – will not believe you when you recite premises (1) through (6), above.

Now, what do you do when people don't believe you? Well, first you ask yourself if *you* really believe you, because you can't fake the passion it takes to sell as bitterly unpopular a set of ideas as these may be right now. My whole career can be summed up in the six words, "When I believed, I was believed." But I'll be the first to acknowledge that the converse was also true.

Having reality-checked your faith and found it in good repair, you could then turn to your unbelieving interlocutor and cordially invite him to go jump in a lake. This is morally and intellectually correct, and it may yet come to this, but it puts no meat upon the table. Herewith, Plan B: If you can't get people to buy your version of what may be about to happen, try getting them to buy theirs.

This process starts, of course, with discovering via the Socratic method what their outlook actually is. Now, the truth is they haven't actually *got* an outlook – not an intellectually formed one, anyway – they're just scared. But since grownups aren't allowed to say they're just scared, people are going to blow a lot of headline-driven smoke at you, trying to convince you that they're reasoning when you both know all they're doing is fearing – wallowing in nameless, numberless terror. And since you can't reason with terror, you have to help people work themselves through it, and thus out of it. With the Dow currently around 8000, that process might sound something like this.

Advisor: OK, you're not crazy about my outlook, such as it is. Let's talk about yours. In your view, where's the Dow going?

Client: Uh, uh...5000.

Advisor: Down, in other words, pretty close to 60% from its peak three years ago.

Client: Sure; easy.

Advisor: Know how many times it's done that in the last hundred years – gone down close to 60%?

Client: No, actually; I don't.

Advisor: Once. In 1929-32.

Client: Huminahuminahumina...

Advisor: This feel like 1932 to you? I mean, 27% unemployment, breadlines, Hoovervilles, "Buddy, Can You

Spare a Dime"?

Client: But I'm only three years from retirement...

Advisor: So you and your bride haven't got more than about 30 years to live. But we can talk about that later. My question was, does this seem like a replay of 1932 to you?

Client: Well, not exactly, but...

Advisor: It doesn't to me, either, but let's assume you're right. The Dow's going to do something it's only done once in 100 years – finish going down nearly 60%. When, do you think?

Client: Huh?

Advisor: When do you see this happening? How long before this cataclysm is complete?

Client: Uh, the rest of this year.

Advisor: Clear. So we're six or eight months and 3000 Dow points from one of the great bottoms of all time – something that happened once in the last century. Am I understanding you properly?

Client: Wait, wait...I haven't thought this all the way through...

Advisor: [Gently] And yet you were pretty sure my counsel was wrong.

Client: Well, it's just that...

Advisor: Hey, we're not arguing, here. We're on the same side. My only interest is in seeing you do what's best for your family in the long run, as comfortably as possible. Now: your view is that the market will be down this year for a fourth year in a row – which it's also only done once in a hundred years, also in 1932 – and then, at 5000...you'll buy it, right?

Client: For argument's sake...

Advisor: Fine, fine. Now, what's your fallback position?

Client: What's that mean?

Advisor: Could you be wrong, how will you know you're wrong, and what will you do when you conclude that you're wrong?

Client: I'm just not following you.

Advisor: OK, say the Dow got to 5700 in October, and stopped going down. Then it turned around and came back up here to 8000. What would you think, and what would you do?

Client: I might, uh…start to think…maybe I missed it.

Advisor: Define "it."

Client: Uh…the bottom, I guess.

Advisor: [Very gently] Right. So you'd buy it at 8000 then, but you wouldn't buy it – not with any fraction of your capital – at 8000 today.

Client: Get out of here. (Or, alternatively: When you put it that way, it starts to not make as much sense as I thought it did.)

Advisor: [If the latter response] Actually, it makes a lot of emotional sense – these are fearful times, you wouldn't be human if you weren't feeling that fear, and waiting for lower prices has certainly worked in the last three years. But it isn't a long-term investment strategy. And, as you see, it puts you under tremendous pressure to be exactly right…which few of us ever are.

Client: Including you.

Advisor: I'm not trying to be right, exactly. I'm trying to get the people who rely on me out of harm's way. Over the years, I've found that that often means doing things that may not seem very easy at the time.

Client: OK, make me an offer.

Advisor: How about: move a third of your capital back into equities here, at 8000. Then another third at, say, 7000. Then, have some fun: hang on to the other third in a money market fund – not in bonds, please – and see how close to 5000 we get.

Client: [Sheepishly] What if we never get to 7000?

Advisor: Uh, oh. Now you're starting to sound like me. The answer is: the second third goes in at 9000, and the last third at 10,000.

Client: Ouch. Why not just put it all in now, at 8000?

Advisor: Do you not realize that that's exactly what I suggested 15 minutes ago, and you about went postal on me?

Reason alone will never overcome fear, but reason sweetened with empathy and good will may carry the day. We know that there's ample good will on your side. This colloquy is a non-confrontational way of finding out if that sentiment is reciprocated.

– *Financial Advisor*, May 2003

HERE COMES THE SUN

I received an e-mail from a subscriber during the second week in March, just before President Bush's ultimatum to the Iraqi regime and the subsequent military incursion.

The writer is an advisor with an older client couple who were about to capitulate out of a perfectly lovely equity portfolio, and go to cash. And this was surely not, at that moment, an uncommon phenomenon. (Indeed, that Sunday night I wrote "Waiting for the Catalyst," which you saw last month, in which I said that some sentiment indicators of bearishness and capitulation were at near-historic extremes.) What makes this particular case so very poignant is that the clients in question are the advisor's parents.

The first quarter of 2003 was marked by as complete a loss of faith as I've ever witnessed. Though all the stock market did was to give up the gains it posted between mid-October 2002 and mid-January 2003 – retreating toward, but ultimately failing to breach, its bear-market lows – this decline *felt* to people like a new leg down to an even deeper abyss.

I believe the market felt so bad because the economy felt so bad: the countdown to war (with a little help from a horrific winter) induced an all-pervading paralysis, visible everywhere from the ISM index to the employment picture to one's own day-to-day anecdotal conversations with other local businesspeople.

Nor was the malaise unique to our clients, I'm sorry to say. My e-mail traffic from advisors turned especially plaintive during this period. The nadir of that trend was an inquiry from an advisor at a very fine super-regional brokerage firm (not, thank heaven, a subscriber) who asked, in effect: tell me again, why do stocks go up?

Then came the "war." And, unlike most things in human experience, the event was far better than the anticipation. For just as we did in Afghanistan in eight weeks what the Soviet Union could not do in 10 years, we did in Iraq in four weeks what Iran could not do in eight years. We obliterated one of the most malignant regimes on earth – a breeder reactor of evil.

There remain terrible problems in Iraq, chief among them the fact that it isn't a country at all, but a gerrymandered hotbed of the most virulent ethnic hatreds (Sunni-Shiite, Kurd-Turk). But there also remains tremendous opportunity: 100 billion barrels of proven oil reserves, with perhaps that much again possible. (Nobody really knows, because for 10 years whatever money the Saddam regime didn't steal went into weapons, not oil exploration/development.) This is good for Iraq, and good for the world: sooner or later, it puts significant downward pressure on oil prices. But that's all beside the point.

The point is that evil failed, the right prevailed, the world is on notice that the only remaining superpower will fight – with awful and terrible efficiency – when talk doesn't work, the single most anxiety-producing uncertainty weighing on America's economy and its stock market is now gone...and it's spring.

Little darling, it's been a long, cold, lonely winter. Little darling, it feels like years since it's been clear.

Here comes the sun.

Now the economy and the markets can get back to fundamentals. And now we, as advisors, can take a long, hard look at ourselves and at our client roster, and assess the true nature (and extent) of the work to be done.

Of the economy and the markets, little need be said. I refer you to the litany of positive factors detailed in last month's "Waiting for the Catalyst," and in the March 31, 2003 *Fortune* cover essay, "The Case for Optimism." I would only stress the obvious point that the paralysis of the winter was a postponement of the inevitable recovery rather than a fundamental deterioration. The IT equipment that business didn't invest in during February will simply be purchased later rather than not at all (as journalism, with its relentless bias for the negative, would have you believe – and as so many investors apparently *did* believe, at S&P 800).

And when the new generation of IT equipment *does* come on line, after this long drought, it will be far more powerful and far cheaper than the Y2K generation it replaces. I expect this to occasion a further surge in U.S. productivity – as how could it not? – making us even more competitive in the world than we are now.

The larger issue, I think, should be: what did we learn about our clients and about ourselves during this bitter winter of our discontent? And what steps must we take for the balance of the year – not to catch up with some dreamlike production goal that was set on New Year's Eve, but to repair the fundamental weaknesses in our practices, and to address our own failings as well.

Quite apart from the very real financial stress you may have suffered in the first quarter, you wouldn't be human if you weren't exhausted and enervated by the relentless cycle of negative "news" and falling markets. (I know I certainly was, and that's pretty rare.) But the question isn't how you felt, but what you did: how did you *respond* to the faithlessness of clients and prospects? Was your faith bolstered by their fear, or was it the other way around? What did you learn about your clients – or, perhaps more accurately, what dark truths about some of them did you find you could no longer deny? (Because, human nature being what it is, an episode like this brings out the worst in most everybody. Just as it brings out the best in the clients whom you've trained right, and who truly "got it.")

During the first quarter, you were given a template – whether you wanted it or not – for building an entirely new, much healthier business model.

Those of you still holding on to the illusion that you could thrive and prosper on portfolio management alone (and almost as an end in itself) found that such a practice is nothing more than a glorified roller coaster, totally out of your control at tops and crashing at bottoms. Those of you who stayed well-diversified within the context of a long-term plan fared (relatively, if not absolutely) better. And those of you who preached faith vs. fear rather than knowledge vs. ignorance – and who didn't grind yourselves up arguing the so-called "facts" with lapsed believers – probably did best of all.

In practice, you may have found yourself having all three of the above experiences at different times, when dealing with different clients. Well and good: that's the template. If you were honest with yourself – and, especially when business is tough, that's a very big "if" – you knew which client was going to turn out which way. The myth of having A, B and C clients is that you take them all, and deal with all of them as best you can. Now you see how corrosive that myth truly is.

You shouldn't have anything but A clients, which I define, irrespective of the dollars involved, as someone who does pretty much what you counsel him to do pretty much all the time, with good explanation but *without argument.*

(So-called B clients aren't clients at all, but *customers*. And C clients are barnacles: they just slow you down and make your boat ugly.)

Not having enough A clients, as the first quarter should have demonstrated to your complete satisfaction, is no reason to keep (much less to accept more) B's and C's. It's a reason to go on a holy crusade to recruit more A's. And there will never again in your career be more orphaned, abandoned and betrayed A clients looking desperately for sound advice (and even moral leadership) than there are in this glorious spring. Nor will you ever be much more likely to be able to clean up their portfolios at advantageous prices than you are now.

Clean up your business, clean up your attitudes and clean up your life. Scrape off the barnacles, sand down the hull, re-finish it with the fastest coatings available, and sail away to the promised land.

Here comes the sun. And I say: it's all right.

– *NMI*, May 2003

WHAT MUST I DO
T O D A Y ?

"If thou workest at that which is before thee, following right reason seriously, vigorously, calmly, without allowing anything else to distract thee, but keeping thy divine part pure, as if thou shouldst be bound to give it back immediately; if thou holdest to this, expecting nothing, fearing nothing, but satisfied with thy present activity according to nature, and with heroic truth in every word and sound which thou utterest, thou wilt live happy. And there is no man who is able to prevent this."

Roman emperor Marcus Aurelius (121-180) from *To Himself* ("The Meditations of Marcus Aurelius") translated from the original Greek by George Long, 1862

HOW TO SUBSCRIBE

Nick Murray Interactive

Nick's newsletter and spot coaching service includes 12 monthly issues for $249. New subscribers receive copies of Nick's books *The New Financial Advisor* and *Simple Wealth, Inevitable Wealth*. Subscriptions include e-mail access to Nick personally – *as time permits* – for spot coaching on specific issues you're facing in your practice.

Visit www.nickmurrayinteractive.com or call Charter Financial Publishing Network at 732-450-8866, ext. 207.

Financial Advisor

Financial Advisor is the monthly magazine created exclusively for advisors by one of the most experienced and respected financial publishing teams ever assembled. *FA* helps advisors manage and grow their practices while assisting clients in aligning their financial and personal life goals. This magazine features Nick's monthly column, "The Master Advisor."

The magazine is free to qualified subscribers. Visit www.financialadvisormagazine.com or call 732-450-8866, ext. 207.